SAIGON RAIN - HANOI MIST

A Trigger To The World!

By

Ly-Miles

This book is a work of non-fiction. Names and places have been changed to protect the privacy of all individuals. The events and situations are true.

ISBN: 1-4107-4137-0 (e-book)
ISBN: 1-4107-4135-4 (Paperback)
ISBN: 1-4107-4136-2 (Dust Jacket)

Library of Congress Control Number: 2003092600

This book is printed on acid free paper.

Printed in the United States of America
Bloomington, IN

1stBooks - rev. 10/10/03

<u>NOTE</u>

This book is based on a true story. All the names of the
individuals, living or dead, in this book have been changed to
protect the innocent. Any similarity to persons outside this book
is purely coincidental.

<u>Acknowledgements</u>

My family experienced the Indochina War along with everyone else in Vietnam, resulting in my successful writing. It is my hope that the book bridges the cultural gap between my American heritage and my native homeland in Vietnam.

<u>Dedication</u>

To my Mother – the Marvel

Mr. William E. A. Heilner

Mr. John W. Barr

All have given their valuable time and love while I have been working on this book for twenty-five years. Your inspiration, morale and financial support have been a blessing to me. I will treasure your teaching values in my heart forever.

Table of Contents

For the past twenty five years I have never stopped working with all the effort I had. I wrote to President Jimmy Carter in the White House about my support of the Human Rights of the President in helping the Vietnamese refugees to find a home here in America. The White House replied to me as follows:

DEPARTMENT OF STATE

Washington, D.C. 20520

March 10, 1978

First Nat'l Bank of Atlanta
Post Office Box 4156
Atlanta, Georgia   30302

On behalf of President Carter, I want to thank you for your message concerning possible American food assistance to Vietnam and Laos, both of which are reportedly suffering rice shortages. We appreciate your interest in this matter.

The Department agrees with a number of international estimates that Vietnam will suffer a rice deficit of as much as one million tons this year. The situation is apparently quite serious.

Vietnam is receiving considerable grain aid and is also drawing upon its foreign exchange to make up the food deficit. While this deficit is in part due to bad weather throughout the country, in the south the Vietnamese Government's dismantling of the traditional marketing systems, its efforts to collectivize agriculture, and general mismanagement are also important factors. Low official paddy prices are an insufficient inducement for farmers to produce more than a subsistence crop. A recently announced policy to push collectivization acts as a further disincentive to South Vietnam's traditional owner-cultivator.

The Administration has no plans to provide food aid to Vietnam. As you may know, U.S. assistance to Vietnam is prohibited under P.L. 480 and other applicable legislation. Moreover, we do not believe there is any wide Congressional sentiment which would be favorable to providing food aid to Vietnam.

The food situation in Laos is becoming increasingly severe, perhaps relatively more severe than in Vietnam. Generally, the same causes that affect rice production in Vietnam are responsible for the shortage in Laos as well.

The Lao Government has not asked us for food aid, but the
United Nations' Development Program (UNDP) has formally
requested international food assistance on behalf of Laos.
The UNDP estimates a rice shortage of 367,000 tons over the
coming 12 months. This figure may be too high, but clearly
a major shortage exists which Lao purchases and foreign
donations have not so far made up.

The Department is actively considering food aid to
Laos. We are now engaged in the necessary groundwork to
decide whether such aid is desirable and feasible. The
decision requires a careful analysis of a number of con-
siderations, including the state of our relations with
Laos. Finally, our decision will require close consulta-
tion with the Congress.

Sincerely,

Hodding Carter III
Assistant Secretary
for Public Affairs and
Department Spokesman

After many years, I wrote a letter to the President at that
time, Mr. George Bush, a petition requesting relocation of my
family to the United States. With my book being published, it
might put my family in danger with the Vietnam government. I
am hoping that my family can be helped from being retaliated
by the government in Vietnam. I wrote:

December 27, 2002

President George Bush % Dept of State Washington, DC

Dear Mr. President,

I know you are a very busy man, and I would like to thank
you in advance for your time and consideration of my petition
and appeal. I had the privilege of working with the United
States in the embassy in Viet Nam during the conflict. I became
a *U.S.* citizen in 1982. This is my country and I have shared
and contributed as a citizen of America. I believe in democracy,

the American Constitution and the Bill of Rights, and have always been willing to support this country and fight for freedom.

I wrote a book about my experiences in Viet Nam during the conflict. It was not easy and it took me a great deal of time and soul searching. The work on my book is complete. My book is in the process of being published and will be distributed worldwide. The title of the book is *Saigon Rain. Hanoi Mist - A Trigger to the World.*

By way of introduction, I am sending you copies of the newspaper articles that have been written about me, a two-page letter to President Carter written in 1978, and a copy of my book for your library. I hope you will enjoy reading my biographical stories. I have been dreaming and hoping to share my stories with the world and I have waited more than 25 years before publishing my works. The publication of the book does create some danger for my family in Viet Nam.

Therefore, I respectfully request that you consider my petition to relocate my family from Viet Nam to the United States where they can live without fear of retaliation from the current government. I am anxiously waiting to hear from you, Mr. President. Please know that your decision will help to save the lives of my 28-member family. Please allow my family to come to the United States and live in the land of the free and the home of the brave.

With much gratitude, your humble citizen,

April Nguyễn
Atlanta, Georgia

I

Destined to America

As the war came to a close and government stability degenerated in Saigon, people who had associated with or worked for America became fearful for their safety. Their fear quickly changed to panic. People, who had lived comfortable lives, suddenly saw all that they had accumulated become worthless to them. It comes as horrible realization that material goods and in many cases friendships, were valueless when society dissolved about them. The only thing of true value is one's life and the freedom as, "One can live in poverty but be rich in spirit."

In an attempt to calm down the confused situation, the government had forbidden all travel and enforced censored of the all war news. Travel within the country was restricted. Security police reinforcements were put on the streets to guard people and their actions. Only foreigners, and people related to them, were free to leave Saigon, if they so desired. People, who wanted to leave, attempted any method to gain an exit from Saigon to safety. Those that did manage to escape Saigon did so under various forms of ruse.

Due to working for Vinnell Corporation and the U.S. Embassy in Saigon, my departure was arranged. I married an American man name André and came to the United States.

One month before my departure from Saigon, I received a letter from a married friend in South Carolina. She was a former embassy employee. Her letter requested that I help her brother and sister get to the States. I performed her request because she was a good friend of mine. So I asked André to assist these two young people. The next person I assisted was Dee, a close girlfriend of mine. She was also a former embassy staff member.

From my home to Tan Son Nhut airport was about six miles. It took me three days to travel these six miles. The first two days after I left home, I stayed in the embassy building. The roof of the building could be used as a helipad in case of an emergency. Due to the siege that was taking place, these were tense and fearful hours. When my friends and I entered the embassy, we had committed ourselves to either freedom or death. Death was certain if we were not rescued before the communist troops took over the embassy compound. Military discipline was disintegrating among the Vietnamese troops. The troops had lost their leaders.

Many Americans in the embassy wept for the bleak destiny of the people and country of Vietnam. Witnessing their sincere emotions affected me deeply.

I needed help leaving Saigon, so I turned to a friend of mine, André that worked at the US Embassy. We arranged a meeting in my diner club and restaurant that I owned in Saigon.

"André!" I cried out gently.

As usual, André was always polite with me, he replied,

"Yes, April? What can I do for you?"

I said:

"I want to go to United States for six months. Maybe after that time everything will be okay, at home in Saigon then I will return home. What do you think?" I declared to André.

André replied with his usual gentleness,

"It is up to you, April. Whatever you want to do, I will go along with you."

I explained to André,

"I do not want to leave home. But, at this point I will not have anything to do until the situation in Vietnam is resolved. I should leave for the United States. Can you get me an American man to marry me and get the necessary exit visa to America?"

André said in a solemn voice,

"Yes April, I will have you sign some papers real soon since you have waited this late to decide that you want to leave. The reason I am still around is to get you out of here before the chaos begins in the Saigon city. I was waiting for you."

At this point, André's usual meekness was gone. He had become a valiant hero who had come to rescue me at the last

4

terrifying days in Saigon. I was overwhelmed by his determination but concealed it inside of me. I said,

"My family and I had a lifelong establishment in this country. We do not wish to leave everything behind such as our relatives and graveyards of our ancestors. My family will remain here, except for me."

André prepared the papers for me to sign. He then asked me to sign all the papers for a family comprised of a father, mother and their two children, ages ten and thirteen. Their last name was the same as mine, so it was easy to claim that they were my family. At first, I refused to sign for their papers. I wryly told André,

"André, do I have a commission from doing the paper for your friends?"

André replied with enthusiasm,

"Yes, Ma'am! Anything you say."

André and I decided to get married so I could bring my other thirteen family members with me. Otherwise, I would be leaving by myself.

After the second day in Saigon, we were told to move to the Defense Attaché Office (DAO) compound at the airport. There we were to receive our papers before proceeding to the States. We had difficulty with the security police at the airport. Prior to entering the airport, André put me and two of my friends in the trunk of the Mercedes so he could get us inside the airport. The police looked in the car but did not look in the trunk.

Prior to leaving, one of the girls asked me to help her boyfriend to leave Saigon. Between my brother and I, we arranged for the young man to escape Saigon. Eventually, this young man became my adopted younger brother in the States. At midnight as I was preparing to depart Saigon; I requested from an embassy employee that he notify my family, particularly my brother. This request was made secretly as all private communications by wire or telephone were forbidden.

When the plane took off we were still not sure we would be safe. The plane could have been shot down, but thank God we made it safely.

Our first stop after Saigon was Clark Air Forces Base in the Philippines. There the American Red Cross welcomed us. There was a group of approximately forty people waiting to meet the plane. These people embraced the evacuees and escorted us to the Red Cross building. There were emergency medical care available for the evacuees, and identification cards were made up.

The behavior of the group of people who represented the United States caused a great emotion of relief in the hearts of the evacuees. We were happy for our safe arrival, but sad because of leaving our country. We were worried about being strangers in a new land. In particular, I was very sad about departing my homeland without knowing if I would ever return. On the other hand, I was glad to gain knowledge of the United States of America.

In 1969, I took a trip to Japan for cultural research study. When I arrived at Haneda Airport in Tokyo, I felt sorry for the people of my war torn country. Japan is also a small country by contrast but a peaceful one. The people and industrial community of Japan were thriving and progressive, while in Vietnam our development was hampered by the continuous war. Many times I wished that I could marry and settle in a country like Japan rather than a country where one could be happily married one day and a widow the next. I could not see bringing children into the world to be without a father, or possibly a mother.

We remained in Clark Air Force Base, Philippines four days before proceeding on to Anderson Air Force Base, Guam. We flew there on a Pan American 747. There we lived in a camp hastily constructed by a U.S. military group comprised of the Air Force, Navy, and Marines. There was a shortage of beds, mosquito netting, showers, toilets, and home cooked food but what a wonderful feeling to be free from communist domination.

I stayed in Guam for two days, and then proceeded to the mainland. The three other younger people who left Saigon with me no longer needed my help as they had relatives in the States.

I left André and my friends in Guam to escort a young Vietnamese wife and her three children to Camp Pendleton in California. She had left her American husband back in Saigon for he feared for their safe departure. André would follow three days later.

A cargo plane flew us on from Guam to the States. It was not insulated and the noisy sounds from takeoff were very loud. Once we were off the ground and cruising at twenty-nine thousand feet, we found that the lack of insulation was like an inexpensive refrigerator. There were seventy-five people on the plane, or should I say seventy-five cold people on the plane. Being a cargo plane, it had the seat straps running down the wall on both side of the plane. I am sure it took several hours to get the frozen seat marks out of our seats. While enroute, we had box lunches and enjoyed the cheerfulness of the Air Force personnel who piloted the plane. There is nothing more enjoyable like watching a group of people leaving a communist dictatorship aboard an unheated plane with cold lunches realizing everyone is heading towards freedom. The plane was our passport from the war zone and we felt like we were on our way to heaven.

What bothered me the most was that my family was not coming to the United States with me. Prior to my youngest brother's death because of the war, there were four brothers in our family; all of them were in the military. My mother was and still is to this day, a minister of the Cao Dai sect, as well as an oriental physician. Cao Dai is a seventy-year-old religion, which believes in God, Buddha, and Jesus Christ. This religion has two million followers based in South Vietnam. As a physician, she cured many people and relieved a lot of pain. As defined by her religious beliefs, she never accepted any money for her services. She believed that her services would bring blessing to her children's lives. My father was a military officer during the French and South Vietnamese government ruling period. Also, my mother's brother was the Chief of Police in Saigon. My parents were loyal to their country. They were raised in Vietnam so they will live and die in their own country.

To me, leaving home did not mean that I was unfaithful to my family or country. I just could not agree with the politics of the incoming government. My love for my family and for my country's culture is faithful, but I now had the wonderful opportunity to go to the United States of America.

When I arrived at Camp Pendleton in California, I met this seventeen-year-old man who eventually became my adopted younger brother. He appeared to me to be a bright young person. Even though I knew nothing about his background, his words to me were deliberate. He appeared to be a well-educated young man. He had the ability to write, speak, and read three Chinese dialects, Vietnamese, and was learning English. He mentioned that he could assist me in translating my writing into Chinese and several other dialects.

Now the United States became my home. Here I could have the freedom that all human beings desire. Having come to the

States, I found a wide cultural gap between my old and new homes. There were many things I did not understand in my new home. Most people from the West do not understand my culture, so I am different to them. These differences have many times caused me to become extremely homesick for my motherland.

After much soul searching, I knew that I could never accept Saigon's communist government. I voted with my feet against the communists when I boarded the plane leaving Saigon for Clark Air Force Base and there was no possible return for me until there would be a change in the communist rule.

Since I was a small child, I believed in personal freedom. My family is the most important thing in my life, but I love freedom. Under the new Vietnam communist government, my personal freedom of thought, spirit, and speech could have me jailed. To me, this is the difference between living and existing.

After I arrived in the United States, André refused to give me my cut. To keep me happy, he only spent a little on me from time to time for the past ten years. He later wanted to marry me truly if I would come to where he lived. I decided not to marry

him for various reasons but mainly for mistrust.

II

Unexpected Reception

André telegrammed his parents of our arrival. At their home in Bloomington, Illinois, his mother made a joke that I was a rice paddy maid who was arriving at her home with her son. Due to some difficulty involving the paper work for the family we brought with us, André had to remain in Guam in order to get that done.

All my clothes in Saigon were tailor made and had ruffles on the shoulders. My white shoes also were made to order. Perhaps in her mind, prior to meeting me at the airport, she was thinking of a typical rice paddy woman with mud on her feet, which she saw on T.V. This was probably what she expected while at the airport.

André's mother picked me up and while in her car, she said with a cool look,

"I thought André brought home a maid to wash dishes for me. But he brought home a princess."

Since I have been dealing with people from all walks of life in my early younger age, I reassured her of my abilities.

"I can do that too. I also can cook and do anything else in the household. I am not only good in public but in the family as well. You will not be disappointed Mrs. Cook."

André's mother comfortably sat back on her driver seat instead of seating with a straight back with tension while steering the wheel. I knew that I succeeded in fooling her with my uneasy feeling about her approach with me. Mrs. Cook complimented me,

"You speak very good English."

In a polite manner, I replied,

"Thank you ma'am. I still have a lot more to learn."

Mrs. Cook was sixty-two years old and very heavy set from the waist down. Her hair was all white with body curls. Despite her age and facial wrinkles, she had a disarming smile just like her son André. Their smiles were identical.

André's father was a farmer who raised corn in Illinois. Having been in the agriculture business for thirty-five years, he was ready to retire. They lived with a grown son, who was twenty-three years old. Their home was one of the most beautiful ones in the town of Bloomington. His young brother was five foot ten inches tall, blonde curly hair, and was a well built and good looking young man. His captivating blue eyes had a glow when they rested on me. Since their mother was concerned about a maid, I offered my help cleaning up the dishes.

After I arrived at my sponsor's family home in Bloomington, Illinois, I received a letter from an old girlfriend who had married a U.S. Army colonel stationed in Vietnam. They settled in northern Maine after returning to the States. Her phone calls and letters said they wanted me to visit them and maybe they could help me locate a job. They wrote to me stating they would

16

meet me sometime later at Boston's Logan Airport, where they were visiting relatives.

André arrived at his parent's home with all my suitcases. He secretly showed his mother a large briefcase full of jewels of Jade and solid gold. This is considered an international currency around the world. Since I was not supposed to see these, it made me feel uncomfortable with André's attitude with his mother. He did not realize I saw him. I was his friend and business partner, not a stranger in his family's home. He showed his mother the jewels in a discreet manner with the intention of not splitting the offerings. The evening came and we sat down and had dinner together. His mother said, in a confident manner.

"April. Why don't you say grace before we eat?"

I was puzzled for a couple seconds because I had never said grace in English before. So I just made up something, something I knew in Vietnamese. I said,

"Bless us our lord and these gifts which we shall receive through you. Amen."

André parents seemed impressed with me. After dinner we gathered together in the den, and talked about the many things back in Saigon. Billy, André's brother, was greatly interested about my background and about how many girlfriends I had back in Saigon. He asked if they looked as nice as me. I was not in the mood of talking because of my travel fatigue and disappointment in André's concealment. But since Billy was so eager to know many things from Vietnam, I participated in the conversation by telling Billy,

"I have many girlfriends back home and they do not look exactly like me. They all looked different. Many of my friends speak English, French, and Chinese. Some of them left Saigon for England, Australia, France and other countries. I came to America because America is one of the most advanced industrial powers in the world. The ambitious person has opportunities in the U.S. that are hard to beat. I want to see the country that everyone talked about."

Billy's smile never ceased, it seemed to be there forever. He appeared so pleased with my presence. He made me blush with his compliments. I covered my face with my hands to attempt to conceal my feelings. At that moment Billy said in a joyful voice,

"Ah, you are blushing! I like your cute manner."

I threw a quick glance at Billy and got out of my chair and I told him,

"With you, I seem never to do wrong. How can I be so perfect unless you are fooling me? André, your brother might not like all these compliments you have given me. I had better go to bed. I have been up early since I left Guam this morning. Good night."

I went to my bedroom and turned out the light. I lay down on my bed and tried to sleep but I could not because everything seemed to happen so quickly. It was hard for me to believe that I was actually in America. Then I asked myself, "What did André tell his parents about me?" Was I his wife or his girlfriend? I needed to find out about this from André. I got out of my bed and tiptoed to the door and looked outside to see if the light was out. I walked to André's bedroom and knocked on his door. André opened the door and stood in his pajamas pants with a bare chest. He had an athletic build. Then André said,

"Yes April?"

I stepped into his bedroom and sat down on his bed. I questioned,

"André, what did you tell your parents about coming home with me?"

He replied,

"I told them in my telegram that I am coming home with a wife."

André answered quickly along with a smile.

"If I am your wife, why do you and I sleep in a separate room? Did not they ask you about that?" I queried.

André explained,

"I told my parents that you came a long way. Therefore, I need to let you sleep for a few days. After a few days, I will find you an apartment so you can have your own place and I will help you get a job."

I inquired,

"Why can't I stay here with your parents for awhile? I am brand new in the States. I do not know anyone or how to get around. How can I manage to be by myself in an apartment?"

André grasped my arms in his hands and said,

"I will be right there with you if you want me to. I will do anything to keep you happy. I know it will take sometime for you to adjust but everything will be okay"

I answered,

"You are our hero. You have brought us to the U.S. We owe you our love and gratitude."

André replied,

"Do not mention it. I did what you wished me to do. I care about you and I could not refuse any of your requests."

21

I explained,

"I am a very assertive woman. I do not mix business with pleasure. Can you tell me if this is business or pleasure?"

André grinned,

"Both, first the business part is to get you and others to the United States. Second, the pleasure is when you fall in love with me."

I laid his hands down from my arms. I told André,

"Good night, André. I will talk to you in the morning."

The next day I went to the shopping mall with André's mother. We spent the first couple hours browsing around and finally I saw a delicate looking dress which was hanging in a shop in the mall. When my eyes rested on the hanging dress Mrs. Cook suggested,

"Do you like that dress? Let us go in and try it on."

We walked in the shop and I tried it on. Mrs. Cook looked at me with the dress on, she complimented,

"The dress is made for you, April. It is very elegant."

Mrs. Cook walked over to the cash register to pay for the dress. I immediately came by her side and politely asked her to let me pay for the dress, I said with affection,

"Mrs. Cook, may I pay my bill?"

Mrs. Cook was very alert,

"I want to buy you a gift, April. Is that alright?"

I replied,

"As you wish. That is a most wonderful gift which I never expected, thank you very much."

We went to several shops and then we sat down at a sidewalk cafe in the mall. It had a hot Ovaltine drink and Mrs. Cook ordered a hot chocolate. Mrs. Cook was very energetic and easy-going with me. We conversed mostly about my shopping pleasures in Saigon. I liked to shop around but only bought after I compared all styles and prices. I said,

"Mrs. Cook, I like to wear good clothes at all times and I also like fashionable styles for the various different occasions. Clothes largely make people. Don't you think?"

Mrs. Cook went along with my ideas,

"Absolutely, we are in a modern society where clothes make a difference. You look good in everything you are wearing. In my case, I am heavy enough to wear only extra large sizes."

After I sipped the last drop of my Ovaltine in the cup, I asked Mrs. Cook to shop with me for a pair of shoes. I said,

"I need a pair of open air white sandals to walk around in this kind of nice weather."

Mrs. Cook agreed,

"Sure, why not! Shall we?"

In the shoe shop I took off my shoes to try on the new shoes while Mrs. Cook's eyes looked at my feet. She suddenly commented,

"You have nice small feet."

"Thank you, I am only five feet four inches tall and weigh one hundred fifteen pounds. Am I small?" I responded.

Mrs. Cook smiled with,

"With delicate feet and hands like yours you can not be a farm girl."

I smiled back with Mrs. Cook,

"You are right about that. If I have to do the farm work, I can do that too."

This time Mrs. Cook also insisted to buy me the pair of sandals. I had no other choice but to accept her gifts. We went back home and I found some coffee spots on the back of my dress. Mrs. Cook asked me to wash my dress because the dress's instructions were to hand washing. I calmly refused,

"Mrs. Cook, please do not do that. I will wash my dress myself later. Right now I just want to take a nap. Thanks for shopping with me."

I went to my bedroom shortly after that. I left my new dress in the living room. About an hour later I woke up and walked down the hallway where the laundry area was. I saw Mrs. Cook holding my new dress in her hand and washing the spots off the new dress. I was terrified and exclaimed.

"Oh no! Please do not do that Mrs. Cook. I feel terrible to let you do the washing for me. I should have not worn the dress."

Mrs. Cook gently looked in my eyes with affection and said,

"Have you rested long enough? You feel better after you have had some rest. I almost finished the washing so let me hang the dress up for you. It is my pleasure, not work. Is that okay?"

I could not argue with her. She was so quick with washing my dress, so I relaxed and thanked Mrs. Cook for her kindness. I just did not want her to think that I was a lot of work for her. Her son André had brought me home to her from Saigon and I did not want to be a burden to anyone.

III

Bait and Vengeance

Later in the day, I received a couple phone calls from Madeline, a girlfriend of mine in Maine. Madeline was married to a Lieutenant Colonel in the United States Army. She met him while he was in the service in South Vietnam. She and I were classmates and friends in junior high school. With a joyous voice, she said,

"Hey, April, I am so glad to know that you are here in the States. As soon as I received your message from Camp Pendleton, California, I called you right away."

Madeline was coy because of her ulterior motive. She wanted to get me involved as mediator between her and her husband. Her problem was an inability to express herself fluently in English. She and her husband had developed a communication gap. Since their marriage in Saigon, I was

27

needed to interpret in English to her husband as to what exactly was bothering Madeline. In this way, she felt secure that he would fully understand her.

She said,

"We are old buddies and I love you like my own sister. I want you to come and stay with us and we will take care of you. You will be our number one guest. There are a number of Vietnamese in Maine that we can be friends with."

Madeline's intensions convinced me. So I though to myself, "The worse that can be for me is to leave Maine if I do not like it there."

I replied,

"Give me a couple of days to book the plane ticket then I will be on my way."

When I arrived in Boston, my friends were not there to meet me. And because of my being in the States for only twelve days, I became quite upset and worried about being stranded in a new city. I had heard that one has to be careful as a single woman in the United States. Fortunately, a representative of Trans World Airline (TWA) said that she knew someone who would help me find my friends in Maine.

I relaxed in the plane leaving Boston, and upon descending into Presque Isle, I looked down at a lovely town. It was late evening on May 12, 1975 and a chilly wind was blowing, and I was very tired from the journey but my first interest was to eat dinner and get some rest.

An elderly couple who were friends of Sam, the Army colonel, picked me up at the airport and took me to their home, where I waited for my friend.

The house was cozy and the owners had numerous pets. I sat at the dining room table and ate dinner. It was a tasteful dinner. The attitude of this couple for some strange reason seemed to resent my arrival and it puzzled me. This situation was a bit of a dilemma to me.

Whether they were really typical Americans or they were the exception to the rule, I did not know. Even though all people may be different, the Vietnamese refugees came to the United States because they had to leave their country to find a new life, and freedom. Many of us lacked the educational background which would allow for a quick adaptation to the American way of life. It would take us time, just as it had others who came before, to adjust to this new found freedom. One can still go to a large American city and find Polish, Puerto Ricans, Ukrainians, etc., that even after many years still have not blended into the mainstream of American life.

Later that evening, they located Madeline and her husband. Madeline asked me to stay with them.

What a shock I had when we arrived at the house. My God! Was this the house my friend had described in letters to her family in Vietnam? She had written about a luxurious home. My eyes saw a huge box, like a cargo container. I did not know what to think. How different it was from the houses of my native Saigon. I had arrived at my destination and spent my visit in their house trailer. Since I was new in the United States, I felt it was convenient for me to stay in their house trailer. I could not relax with Madeline and her husband. My stomach was in pain from the unexpected occurrence at the airport in Boston.

I realized why my old girlfriend and her husband did not show up at the airport in Boston for two reasons: (one) her sister, whom I had brought to the United States, had promised to reimburse me with the money I spent in getting her here; (two) I repeated that Cyrano De-Bergerac by composing all of Madeline's letters that she sent to her boyfriend. She really wanted him for her husband. Before she married, I faked dozens of letters for her to see if they could get together. He was a high ranking officer with the American Army in South Vietnam. She met him through my connections, where I worked as a manager with the Combined Recreation Association (CRA) of the American Embassy Club. He returned home to the United States. He was not able to marry Madeline because he was already married to an American lady and had five children. Madeline and I were able to convince him with my phony letters to get him to return to Saigon to marry Madeline. We used a false statement concerning her becoming pregnant by him, to arouse his fatherly instincts. She felt that the love alone would not be enough for him to divorce his wife. So she concocted the pregnant story. He fell for it and divorced his wife and then came to Saigon with loving arms to claim his bride and child. Madeline was overwhelmed with the joy of winning her man.

To back up her story about "their" baby, she secretly got in touch with an agency and adopted a baby girl. So when he arrived in Saigon, he saw her with the baby. As time went on during their new life together in United States, Madeline experienced guilty feelings about the fraud. She always felt tension about their relationship and my presence only made it worse with the fear that I might reveal her secret. This was why she left me stranded at the airport.

Madeline seemed to know what was going through my mind and she brutally cut me to pieces, she said,

"April, set your suitcase down and relax. You are home at last instead of out in the cold snow of April. Maine winter is very long lasting, about six months and it can kill people who do not get used to it." (I felt she was out to get me.)

She said,

"I meant the cold of Maine winter." (Like hell, she wanted my neck.) "This is a no-man's land and your actions are in grave danger." (Her husband still did not catch on about Madeline. I sensed my life was in mortal danger.) "After sometime, we will have to find you a man, who can feed you. We only can feed you so much and so many days here." (Boy, did she hate me) "Back home, you always seemed to do better than most of us with money and fame."

She must have been jealous of me and now was her chance to get even with me. I was the "big cheese" in Saigon. Now she was the big cheese married to a colonel and I was at her mercy. There was no one to protect me. I left all my worldly goods and twenty-eight family members in Saigon. I had one of the largest and most popular nightclubs in downtown Saigon. Now all I had was a few bags, twelve to be exact, of beautifully tailor made beautiful clothes and even made-to-fit underwear! But I was forced to leave everything in Saigon. I lost a fortune. Underneath the surface, she had hated my guts in Saigon. At that time I had everything and she felt way below me. I never realized how she fiercely resented me.

She continued,

"But, what seems to be a problem is that you are not on your own."

(Now was her chance to butcher me - do me in)

"I hated your success and power back home. We went to the same school and graduated together but why did you have the bright side and my side was so bleak in Saigon. However, you are at the end of the United States borders here in the wilderness with great danger in all directions. You might as well decide this is your burial ground, right here in Maine."

I felt a cold shiver all over me from her personal attack on me and this only added numbness along with the long journey to Maine. I knew I should not say the wrong things in that present circumstance. I was like a bird in a cage, I responded to her,

"I have had hard times in my life before. It was just because you were not near me always for you to understand that I also had my ups and downs. During the war in Vietnam, my youngest brother died at seventeen in the battle in Laos for the sake of peace for all of us. There were times when I experienced great pain with my family but usually I did not show it."

(I needed to cool her down so I might be able to get out of this place with my life. I had to say something to work on her sympathy.) I calmly said,

"I will get along on my own and I will not be a burden to you. I need a few days to get myself together. I am very grateful to you."

Madeline for the moment seemed not too up tight, but she still was skeptical about our secret of the baby. She blurted out,

"Sam already knew about the father of the baby and it does not matter to him. As a matter of fact, he loves me better now because I did it for the great love I have for him. I know you have done so much for me, even though during those high school years many more young men were after you than me. But you did not make a big deal out of it. Then one day I fell for a guy who was going to graduate from a Technical School in Saigon. But he proposed to you. He was so good looking but you still helped me get him. I hate you for being able to do this for me. I could not do this myself, we were so young. I hate you. You had all those benefits in life without trying so hard."

(I never for a moment was aware of all the power she believed I had with my youthful beauty and influence. She made me realize that she felt I was her enemy. All the good I thought I did was now maybe my downfall)

Madeline talked about our earlier Saigon close relationship. I could say nothing to relieve her hostility. She was not letting loose! She continued,

"What would you do if somebody owed you money and they did not want to pay you back? And remember you are in the United States and in somebody else's home on the edge of eternity. You will leave your belongings here. They are not yours anymore."

(What does she want from me, my life or my belongings? She had me puzzled. What is going to happen next?)

Fortunately, André had almost all my twelve suitcases back in Bloomington, Illinois. I meticulously explained to Madeline,

"I do not worry about the money I loaned to someone, because if they needed the money they can keep it. I do not stop helping others because of one incident and I believe that the good guys will win in the end anyway. This is the way my mother taught me by her example and love. I knew no other way. It was my mother's upbringing that gave me inner beauty and class."

Madeline appeared all worked up from what I said. Her looks became grim and she said,

"Let us see how good a guy is with a knife at his throat or as a car runs over him. There are various avenues to get rid of somebody in this no-man's land. Anybody that comes here to

Maine is at the end. You might as well be prepared for this now."

(Does she really plan on killing me? I thought in my heart that she was such a good friend. How wrong I was. I never dreamed back during my glorious days in Saigon, with all that success, money, and fame that I might end up this way.)

At this point, I did not see any benefit by continuing that negative conversation with Madeline. I started looking at some magazines in the living room. Madeline made some phone calls to her friends at Loring Air Force Base. They were Vietnamese that were married to airmen at the airbase. Madeline was not alone. She was in a position as a ring leader to get the group of Vietnamese wives married to other GI's in Maine to go against me. Some of those also resented my success in Saigon!! In this way, it gave them a chance to get back at me, so they foolishly thought. Madeline had gathered with the group, and together I feared they were out to destroy me. I thought they would take me out in the wilderness and leave me at the mercy of the elements of Maine's dangerous uninhabited area. In Saigon, she felt I was the Goddess and in control of my life. But now in Maine it was her ballgame!!

After traveling from Bloomington, Illinois all day long and arriving in Maine late in the evening. I dropped unconscious on Madeline's couch. She kept talking but I passed out from exhaustion.

The next day, Madeline brought me to meet those Vietnamese American couples. As we arrived at one of the airman's home, the Vietnamese wives gathered together with Madeline to plot my downfall. One of the wives of an airman, who looked skinny and frail remarked, looking at me,

"This is a no-man's land and whoever comes here must remember that they could loose their life at anytime." She snarled,

"Big wheels do not exit around here. If we hear something we do not like, we will just eliminate the problem, whatever it takes!!!"

At that point, I felt I needed to fight for my survival but at the same time I needed to keep my cool. I needed to say something that would interest these women and help myself out of their critical onslaught. I then said,

"This is a no-man's land, and all of us are here at the end. The United States is a large ocean and we are the small Vietnamese boat; we need each other. We need to be industrious and better ourselves in this place. Together we will win, but divided we will loose. Success does not have to have a lot of money. We can grow from a small business like production to a large factory such as making beads, custom jewelry or possibly macramé. Those items would take only a small amount of investment. As the business continues to grow, our investment could grow."

Suddenly Madeline and the others beamed with bright glow in their faces. My remedy seemed to influence their need for success. A heavy set woman in the bunch shouted out,

"She has a good idea, which could keep us busy and make us money. In that way we would not have to depend on our husbands. April was successful in business in Saigon before and that is what makes her idea sound good!"

Kim was the woman whom agreed with me. She spoke to me so Madeline and others could hear,

"We all have lived in this situation for years and never thought of doing something like that. Now, April is new from Saigon and gave us the idea. Why don't we start thinking of ways to make some money to better our lives and our families in Vietnam."

The group of Vietnamese wives appeared to be excited by the suggestion I made. One got up from the table and others followed preoccupied by this idea of their going into their own business. Anyhow, by making this constructive plan, they all diverted their attention to it rather than to me, except that is for Madeline. She looked confused with my approach. The other wives suddenly lost interest in decapitating my head and feeding me to the wolves in the Maine back country.

Madeline did not like this new development. They no longer were out to get me. They did not depend on Madeline for leadership and guidance. I was not concerned too much about Madeline then. She was cut down to size by her own group. I now felt a great relief and actually saw the group of Vietnamese wives as not my adversaries but my comrades. But, I could see Madeline remained my adversary.

As we arrived back at her home later that evening, Madeline said,

"Sam likes your firm butt. He said, you have a good looking behind. Are you horny? Since you loaned me the money to get my sister here, I can loan you my husband. Go ahead to his bedroom, he is alone by himself. You and I are like sisters to each other. Do not worry about me here, go on:"

Madeline's malice was quite obvious to me, not to her husband. She could not turn or twist me around. She wanted me to fall in her trap. Perhaps she thought I would be on my knees begging for her mercy. When she made that proposition, I felt the poisonous venom dripping from her lips. Something

42

about her, even in Saigon, never gave me full trust with her. In our childhood, she never seemed to level with me. When she had a love affair with my first husband, she concealed it and was not truthful with me. She always desired my men, as though she needed my blessing by having my admirers. She met my first husband the previous year. Even a year later, her goal was to get him. Fortunately this did not upset me greatly, because I was leaving my first husband anyway. However, I was disappointed with her. After all, I believed we were such close friends, such as the sister I never had. Sadly I could never move her to tell me the truth about her and my first husband. She waited too late to tell me something I already knew. What a sadness she brought to me. Madeline was not a true friend. Her hatred of me went back to my success in Saigon.

I remember a time in Saigon long ago. I was a restaurant manager of seventy-five employees at the American Embassy Club. I arranged to allow her and her Colonel, who was only her boy friend at the time, to have dinner at that exclusive, elite restaurant. Entrance was by invitation only. Only members or their guests could come and he was not a member. It was open exclusively to the highest ranking individuals of the American Embassy, their friends and their family. Everyone else was excluded. The next day when they saw me, instead of appreciating me for this favor I arranged for them, Madeline sarcastically said that the food caused them to get sick. I managed the restaurant so I knew better. She resented my position. I should have then realized that she was very jealous of my job. This time I confronted her stating,

"No, Madeline. I am alright. Sam is your loving husband. I could not do that at all and it is against my standards. If you asked me to clean the house or cook for you I would gladly do that. You have been good to me to let me stay in your home and that is more than I could ask of anyone."

My confrontation with Madeline this time resulted with a different side of her — one that was soft and tender. She gently advised me of where I could get a blanket, and where the bedroom was. She said,

"April, if you do not have enough covers, please let me know. I will get some more for you. I just do not like the idea of you having so much luck in life back in Vietnam. But you ran out of luck with no one here to help you. So you need a hand from an old friend and you know I am here to help you."

Madeline granted me some relief with saying good night in a gentle manner. She finally seemed to cool down with her present mood.

As I lay down on the bed, my eye lids closed and in a short while I was sleeping. My bedroom was normally Sam's office, where he conducted his insurance business.

A week later, Madeline and Sam told me to fix myself up. His boss, a manager of the Lisbon Mutual Life Insurance in Bangor, Maine, was coming to Caribou and planned to take us to dinner that night.

Madeline appeared to cool off or was she faking it? Something in her voice left me wondering "fix myself up?" The tone of her voice made me feel doubtful about her intentions. I was not in a position to make any waves. I was waiting for Madeline to make the right move, so at the right time I safely relocate from their house trailer. Then Madeline said with an artificial tone,

"April, we have been arranging for a week with this meeting with Adam. He is Sam's boss. We think very much of you. Adam is a nice guy. With your background, you ought to meet someone like Adam, not the airmen at the airbase."

For the first time during that last week, I saw Madeline's warmth return slightly. But I still felt tension. To cover those inner thoughts of fear, I replied,

"Thanks, Madeline. You are mighty kind. I wish to repay your kindness."

While in the kitchen, Sam stated,

"Adam is a good boss. He is married and has two grown children. If you are nice to him, he might get you a job."

The first time, back in Saigon, when I saw Sam, he always appeared rather plain and simple. I never could understand what Madeline saw in him. He reminded me of comedian character, "Gomer Pyle" of the television series. We got the show televised in Saigon. Sam eventually retired from the Army and works as a salesperson for an insurance company in Caribou.

Madeline must have read my mind and said,

"Sam is very soft and gentle most of the time. But when he kills domestic rabbits for food, he holds the rabbit in one hand and with the other hand gently caresses the rabbit, and then suddenly, with a butcher knife, he chops the head off. And of course with his usual gentleness, he skins the rabbit instantly. We love those rabbits and he seems to kill them without hesitation."

I was petrified in my seat, when I heard Madeline's description of her husband's killer instinct with the rabbits. I began to feel that Sam enjoyed killing. Maybe that is why he made a career of the Infantry. He was taught to kill in the war for the same reason, I thought. This greatly increased my worry

47

while at their house trailer. I felt sick to my stomach and was so ill that I had to run to the bathroom to throw up.

Madeline, Sam and I left for the Hilltop Hotel to meet his boss. We arrived at the hotel and went to the restaurant lounge where we were to meet Adam. Adam was a medium sized man, maybe five foot nine inches and was a little heavy. He pulled a chair at his table for me, and we all sat down. Sam introduced Adam and in a humorous manner, he said,

"This was the big shot in Saigon that I told you about, Adam. She was the American Embassy Club Restaurant manager."

Adam was also a retired Colonel. He worked for the Lisbon Mutual Life Insurance Company. Adam was Sam's boss. I realized at that moment that not only did Madeline resent my higher level in Saigon, but her "Gomer Pyle" husband also did not like it. Because of his tone of voice while introducing me to his boss, the cynical manner of Sam blatantly labeled me a big shot. Adam, who was in many ways similar to Sam, said,

"Oh, do not worry! I will handle this nicely. I will show April that retired Army Colonels are good company."

Sam and Madeline appeared satisfied about the get together with Adam. As we finished our drinks, Sam and Madeline got up and said goodbye. Madeline leaned over and told me Adam would escort me home.

Alone with Adam, he patted my hand on the table, and said,

"Everything is alright, just have a drink and tell me about yourself, and what you want in the future. I might be able to help you. But if worse comes to worse, would you mind working in the drycleaners?"

I said,

"I do not mind. I just can not wait to get back on my feet and get on my own."

Adam grinned and said,

"I left my notebook in my hotel room — let us go get it?"

Now his true intentions became apparent. I told him I would wait for him in the lounge. He then said,

49

"Let us go and buy a sexy night gown for you."

He handed me a twenty dollar bill and said,

"Here is some bus fare."

I was embarrassed and refused it. I said,

"I wish to pay my own way."

He insisted that I keep the money and after a few moments of passing the twenty dollar bill back and forth on the table, the other diners began to look at us out of the corners of their eyes. This was unexpected and I told Adam I did not need his money. I rapidly lost what little respect I originally had for him. I misunderstood his intentions earlier. His class and polish suddenly disappeared. It was difficult for me to see how he decided that he could buy me unless that intention had been put there by Madeline. In spite of the anger that I concealed in myself, my mother's teaching of nonviolence reminded me that I could accomplish a nonviolent action to avoid violence. I asked Adam to drop me home or I would leave the hotel by foot. That was the last and only time I encountered Adam.

Madeline and Sam were disappointed at the outcome of the "setup" blind date for me. They put him up to this because they believed it would help Sam with his career at the Lisbon Mutual Life Insurance Company.

IV

New Found Hope

While on the plane traveling from Boston, Massachusetts to Presque Isle, Maine I met a lady. She was the Director of the University of Southern California at Loring Air Force Base's Education Center. After I talked with her about myself, Mrs. Eileen Reid gave me her office phone number and asked me to give her a call when I arrived at Caribou, Maine.

I walked outside the house trailer to get some fresh air and also to look for a pay phone, nearby. I found a phone booth at an isolated gas station within walking distance. I dialed the number Mrs. Eileen Reid gave me. The phone rang twice and I heard a voice at the other end say,

"This is the University of Southern California, Mrs. Reid speaking."

I was very happy to hear her voice. I replied,

52

"Mrs. Reid this is April. How are you? We met on the plane from Boston to Presque Isle two weeks ago and you asked me to give you a call."

Mrs. Reid then said,

"Please come into my office, we will talk about you working here."

I anxiously asked her,

"When can I come to see you?"

Mrs. Reid replied,

"Today! This afternoon!"

I responded enthusiastically,

"I am coming to see you now, but I do not know how far I am from you."

Mrs. Reid asked,

"Where on earth are you?"

I said,

"I am at the Trailer Park East."

Mrs. Reid said,

"It is about five miles from where you are. You come to the security gate of Loring Air Force Base and call me. I will drive to the gate and pick you up."

I walked to the gas station office and asked the gas attendant the direction to Loring Air Force Base. I then asked him,

"Is there any taxi cab service in the area?"

The attendant said,

"Not in this area. Everybody that lives here has their own transportation."

It was then one o'clock in the afternoon. I began walking to Loring Air Force Base, which was approximately five miles away. It was a long walk. There were no houses that I passed on the way. Highway One was the only road to her location. But I was hoping my luck would change. Fate was now to tell the tale. My fate had me at his mercy. When I think about the unpleasantness and the thought of my sudden demise I walked jubilantly with enthusiasm to meet Mrs. Reid. Arriving after two hours walk, I called Mrs. Reid at the gate to come to pick me up.

Mrs. Reid said,

"I am so happy to see you. I was thinking that you were doing alright. Why did not you call me before this?"

I did not want to go into details about my problem with my girl friend, so I said,

"I had some business to take care with my girl friend and in past two weeks, she and her husband could not help me to get a job. So I called you up."

Mrs. Reid said,

"How can you find a job in the middle of nowhere? Your friends live in a remote area."

I agreed,

"You are right. I walked five miles and did not see any house on the way here."

Mrs. Reid said,

"My husband and I live in Limestone, about thirteen miles from the Air Force Base. My husband is a farmer and was Dean of Ricker College but now he prefers to work on the farm. It does not bother me, we like living in a small town like Limestone. Sometime later you can come and see us at our home."

When Mrs. Reid and I arrived at the Education Center, she took me over to the office of Mr. Eugene Heston who was the Chief of Staff of the Education Center at Loring Air Force Base. Mr. Heston greeted me by waving his hand for me to sit down. Mr. Heston said,

"Mrs. Reid told me that you need a job right away. What you could do for this office is to make five appointments a day with the military personnel to encourage them to attend the school. Other duties would be to keep student records straight and keep order with the files. Your job title would be Assistant Education Advisor at the Educational Education Center. You will be working directly for Mr. William Forsyth."

Mr. Forsyth shook hands and said,

"I am pleased to meet you."

Mr. Heston continued,

"April, can you start to work here tomorrow morning? Is there anything else we can help with?"

I was touched and deeply grateful to all of the staff of the Education Center at Loring Air Force Base. I did not want to bother them. But, at the time they were the only ones who could help me. I then said,

"I need to get a small apartment as soon as possible."

Mr. Forsyth said,

"I know a high school teacher in Caribou who has a one bedroom apartment in his home for rent."

The teacher, Mr. Ronnie Benfield, is a single parent and has an eleven-year old son. I can call him and make an appointment for you."

Mr. Heston inquired,

"It is eleven miles from Caribou to here. How will you get here April?"

Mr. Forsyth said,

"I have two vehicles, April. You might as well use one for now until you can get yourself transportation."

Things happened so quickly that I did not believe it was for real. My miserable days with my girl friend had suddenly ended this afternoon by finding myself a peaceful place to stay and a job all at the same time.

Mr. Heston evidently read my mind and he comforted me by saying,

"Do not worry April. At least we can get something going for you right now. Anything else we will worry about later. Mrs. Reid will not mind taking you to Caribou to help you to get an apartment."

Mr. Heston was not only the Chief of Staff, but also the Financial Controller of the Education Center on Loring Air Force

Base. He was able to cut back some other expenses to pay me a salary.

We arrived at the home of Mr. Ronnie Benfield. He greeted us at the door and said,

"Please, come on in. Mr. Forsyth called me and I have been expecting your arrival."

Mrs. Reid introduced herself and me to Mr. Benfield who had the apartment. Mrs. Reid went right the subject and said,

"April is from South Vietnam and going to be working with us at the Education Center in Loring Air Force Base starting tomorrow. She needs an apartment to move into this evening. Is your apartment available?"

Mr. Benfield said,

"Yes, Mrs. Reid. I am a teacher myself. I am teaching at the high school in Caribou. I need a good tenant to live here in my home, because I have a small boy who is going into the sixth grade. Anybody I put in must be a good person."

Mrs. Reid inquired,

"What is the rent?"

Mr. Benfield answered,

"The rent is one hundred twenty-five dollars a month including utilities. Since you are from the Education Center, I would waive the deposit."

Mrs. Reid asked me,

"April, do you have the money?"

I happily said,

"Sure, I have the one hundred twenty-five dollars. Mr. Benfield, I am grateful to you for letting me have the apartment. I promise to be a good friend to your son and a good tenant."

I then went back to the trailer with Mrs. Reid to get my belongings. With the help of Mrs. Reid, I moved out of Madeline and Sam's house trailer that evening. Those tense and dangerous moments with my old classmate and friend fortunately had peacefully ended. The presence of Mrs. Reid with me overwhelmed Madeline and Sam. They respectfully followed Mrs. Reid's instructions. Mrs. Reid said to get all my belongings. Since Sam was conducting his insurance business mostly with the military personnel at Loring Air Force Base, he responded quickly to Mrs. Reid's request. Sam knew that Mrs. Reid was in an influential position at the Base. He was not about to disregard Mrs. Reid's wishes. She held a prestigious job and earned the respect of everyone.

God is mighty, and Madeline's marriage did not last. She was divorced sometime later and I never said a word to anyone about anything. Shortly after she abandoned me at the Logan Airport, I heard they had a blood test and it brought out that the baby was not his. So maybe that was the major factor for their separation.

My stay with Madeline and Sam ended in only two weeks. It was a sad house, like something was dying. My old classmate and friend had changed. Her opinion of life and people had the mark of someone who had experienced an evil life. She had difficulty finding her place in this new culture. Largely I believe due to the language barrier and to live truthfully. Most of her new friends were somewhat crude and of low morals. They were unaware of these differences between American culture and Vietnamese traditions. She confided in me about her marital difficulties. She had witnessed her husband's unfaithfulness on a number of occasions and it deeply grieved her. She had become quite depressed about this. It also became obvious that my presence did not bring the joy she had hoped for.

I was sad and found her words empty and left me wondering if I had made a mistake in following the invitation to visit her in Maine.

After I moved out of my friend's home, I then wrote to Adam and told him,

"Sometimes the wealth of man allows him to believe that his wealth is a source of power. I have never looked down on or disrespected any person for his feelings or beliefs.

"People throughout the world are not different. There are fine people and there are others. The difference between our countries is mainly land size. Not only land size, but the size of understandings and concepts. The Vietnam War lasted for twenty-two years. This war was the source of unhappiness for people, a great restriction of their freedom, and had caused many sad things for everyone of my country. The United States is a free country. People here have liberty and freedom which my people had less of.

"In my opinion, Americans are proud of the United States. For this reason, Americans do attempt to understand the feelings of others.

"In Vietnam, as in other parts of East Asia, poverty and lack of education caused severe differences in lifestyles. The Vietnamese culture taught over the past four thousand years to avoid violent action. My mother taught us children to overcome life's difficulties with patience, gentleness, and to respect others."

NOTE: Adam died from a heart attack a year later. His wife died two months after his death.

V

New Fraternity

My first week on the job was very rewarding and happy. With setting up five good appointments of potential students a day, I did well.

I arrived at the office of the Education Center at eight thirty in the morning, and as usual, I picked up the personnel roster at the desk of Mr. Forsyth and went back to my desk and started to call those on the roster to make an appointment. I picked up the phone and started dialing the numbers. During the course of phoning, I occasionally spoke with some USAF men who were married to an oriental, from the Far East. One young Sergeant asked me,

"Miss, you have an accent. Where are you from?"

I answered,

"I am from South Vietnam and I have not been here long."

In a friendly voice the Sergeant said,

"Wonderful! You are a rescued star from the orient. You are working at the Education Center to let those ignorant American wives see that women from Asia are not stupid. My wife is from the Philippines and she has had a hard time getting along with these women at Loring Air Force Base. She could not work in the office like you. But works as a waitress at the NC0 club."

I replied,

"This is a small area of the United States. I am sure there are many more individuals like myself that are working for larger organizations. Working in a restaurant is not degrading. To be a good individual and honest is more important. You love your wife and she loves you — the heck with the others."

The Sergeant replied,

"I know that! But, at times these wives at Loring Air Force Base picked on my wife, and that makes me fighting mad. They like to gossip about my wife saying that she was short, stupid, and maybe a whore at some local bar in South East Asia."

I explained,

"That is okay It is their opinion only! You and your wife are content and live a happy, normal life. In that way she would be able to show others that they were wrong about her. And you too, teach her to speak more English to communicate with American friends. I wish you good luck Sergeant."

After one month on the job, I became a popular subject amongst some of the USAF personnel, especially the B-52 pilots.

One week out of every three weeks, all the B-52 pilots and co-pilots had been on alert to practice their military duties. Hundreds of pilots gathered together in two unoccupied large buildings. This time, many of these officers talked about the presence of a beautiful oriental young woman working in the Education Center on the Air Force Base.

A co-pilot of a B-52, Lieutenant Brady said,

"Who is that pretty girl from the orient working at the Education Center?"

A navigator pilot, Lieutenant Stevenson answered,

"She is from Vietnam and recently arrived in the United States. I wonder if she is married."

Lieutenant Brady responded,

"I am married, but I would sure like to take her out if I was not married"

The navigator answered,

"I do not see her wearing a marriage ring. She might be single. But if she is single, then what the hell is she doing in Northern Maine, a cold place like the North Pole!"

Lieutenant Brady said,

"Since you are single, why do not you take her out and find out more about her?"

The navigator pointed out,

"She is working for the Education Center and she is keeping all the student's records. If things go wrong with her I could be in serious trouble. She is not there just to look pretty. She is there to do her job. I could not take her out and drop her like I did with other girls I had met at each Air Force Base."

Another pilot said,

"You are a butterfly everywhere you go. Now suddenly you are talking about moral values:"

Gus stated,

"I planned to sponsor some Vietnamese and very soon they will arrive in Maine. I am going to ask Miss. April to be our interpreter, because these Vietnamese do not speak much English. Anyone who wants to know about her must stand in line and wait behind me, I am first."

One in the group blurted,

"We will see. You sound like a winner already. We hope she will not stand you up, so the line will not be too long for us."

They all laughed loudly together.

Two months went by and the fund which Mr. Heston arranged ran out. The job he created had ended. Therefore I had to find a new job. Mr. Heston called me in his office and said,

"We ran out of the funds to pay you. But we can get you a job with Mr. Ben McDonald, who is the Dean of the Presque Isle Community College. His office is also here at the Education Center in Loring Air Force Base. You will be his Secretary and by working with Mr. McDonald it allows you free schooling here. There are many courses that you can take at the school in Presque Isle."

I answered,

"Wonderful! When can I start with Mr. McDonald?"

Mr. Heston said in a friendly manner,

"When the end of May comes, you will be working at the office of Mr. McDonald. We will have Mr. McDonald come over here to meet with you. I am his boss, and I write his merit evaluation every six months with the Board of Education. Let's give him a call and we will all meet here in my office."

Mr. Heston was a good hearted man and a good friend to me. Not only in a professional standpoint also was a good human being. He was in charge of all the staff at the Education Center of the base.

After lunch, Mr. McDonald came over and we both met with Mr. Heston in his office. Mr. McDonald said,

"April, your job with me is about the same as before, except you do not have to have five appointments a day. But you should enroll as many students as possible and inform the military personnel of any new courses offered by the school. We are representing Northern Maine Vocational Technical Institute, which is located in Presque Isle, about twenty-five miles from Loring Air Force Base. You could start your new job on the first of June, which is one week from now."

Mr. Heston said

"Good luck, April. You still come to see us. Will you?"

June first came and I moved to the office with Mr. McDonald at Northern Maine Vocational Technical Institute. My job kept me busy most of the time. There were numerous military personnel signing up for new courses. After two weeks, a young B-52 Air Force captain came to my office to see me. I was acquainted with him from the previous office, where I handled his records before and had attended the University of Southern California. This captain greeted me and asked,

"Miss, could I have a few minutes with you?"

I replied,

"Sure Captain, how can I help you?"

Since he thought I did not recognize him, he said,

"I am Captain Gus Blackwell. I am going to sponsor four Vietnamese from the South Vietnamese Navy. But they speak very little English. We need an interpreter for our communication. Could you be our interpreter?"

The Captain overwhelmed me by his good intention in helping my fellow country men. I said,

"With pleasure, Captain. I will be your interpreter. Just let me know when they arrive in Maine. Then I will go with you to

71

the airport. But try to get them here sometime on Saturday or Sunday or else later in the evening, so I will not have to leave my job."

Gus said,

"Please, just call me Gus. I am going to make a phone call to the camp at Guam to make arrangements for the four Vietnamese so they can arrive at the airport in Presque Isle this Saturday afternoon. Can you go with me to pick them up?"

I said,

"Of course I can."

Gus continued,

"There are two camera men. They are from the local newspapers and want to take pictures of the arrival of the Vietnamese and get their story which will be published in their newspapers. I just want to let you know to prepare you for it."

Saturday came and Gus and I arrived at the airport in Presque Isle. We waited about thirty minutes. Then the plane landed with the four young men. Two camera men from the

72

local news papers were there also. The moment we saw them, was for me a very touching moment. They were not only my fellow countrymen, but war heroes. In particular, Gus felt thankful for their plane's safe arrival. Their names were Captain Chiêm Khén, Lieutenant Hiếu Văn Đoàn, Lieutenant Chuẩn Văn Trinh and Sergeant Nguyên Văn Nguyễn.

The reporters took pictures and briefly interviewed the four young men, and I was the interpreter. The reporter of the Star Herald newspaper at Presque Isle questioned all four men with,

"How do you feel upon your arrival here?"

(I acted as the interpreter.)

Captain Chiêm Khén Answered,

"We are extremely excited and relieved to safely be here!"

The reporter of the Aroostook Republican and News of Caribou questioned,

"Do you feel sad to have left your homeland?"

One of the four replied,

"Yes, we left our families behind but in return, we have gained the freedom of being in the United States of America, and hopefully when we can our family will join us."

The reporter of the Star Herald Newspaper questioned,

"What plan do you have or what would you like to do in Maine?"

Captain Chiêm Khén modestly stated,

"We want to get a job and learn the English language, because communication is very important."

The reporter continued,

"Would you accept any kind of work or do you have a particular job in mind?"

Captain Chiêm Khén answered,

"We are trained soldiers to survive in any circumstances. So we would accept any kind of work to give us independence."

The reporter of Aroostook Republican and News questioned,

"What was your experience like when you were on your ship in the ocean attacked out at sea by the Vietnamese Communists (VC)?"

Captain Chiêm Khén said,

"We did not think that we were going to make it until the American submarine came to our rescue. Our ship was sinking from the attack of the VC, and for many days we were lost and drifted in the ocean. The ship went on endlessly at sea because our ship was severely damaged from the shelling of the VC"

The same reporter questioned,

"How did you feel when you realized the Americans found you just before going down?"

Captain Chiêm Khén answered,

"We are thankful to the United States Navy submarine who were our heroes and saved us from the sea. Because of them, we are in the land of freedom. We feel safe here!!"

Same reporter questioned,

"How do you feel about April, your fellow country woman interpreter?"

Captain Chiêm Khén said with a warm smile and looked at me,

"We are glad to have a beautiful Vietnamese interpreter here who speaks our feelings in English."

The four turned to me and one said,

"You are much prettier than we thought. Gus said you were attractive and super sharp. Your hair, your dress and your looks in word is wonderful!

I blushed from their nice compliment and I warmly said,

"Thank you, but you are the ones who are so wonderful and are everyone's heroes."

The reporter shook hands with all of us and wished the best for the four young men. Gus and I got in the car with the four young Vietnamese and headed for Limestone, Maine.

Gus had purchased a home near the base. It was a three bedroom house and he paid seventeen thousand dollars. It was a house for the four refugees and him. Prior to that time, Gus was living on the Air Force Base. I was their interpreter and mentor.

We arrived at Limestone later that afternoon. It is a small town of about two hundred population. Gus stopped at a grocery store for some provisions. We bought groceries to make dinner that night and breakfast the following morning. Chiêm Khén, Hiểu, Chuẩn and Nguyên were always cheerful around us. The four young Vietnamese seemed to sincerely like us. They liked Gus and I well enough that they did not have to hide their happy feelings.

Gus parked the car in the driveway and we all walked into the rear entrance to the kitchen. We sat the grocery bags on the counter and started cooking dinner.

The four young new arrivals helped in the kitchen by cleaning the vegetables, and assisted with making the salad. Gus was watching the news on the television.

One of the four refugee sailors, Hiểu inquired,

"April, have you been in Maine long?"

I answered,

"I have been here since April this year. I am also a new arrival just like you fellows arriving now in Maine. I have been here just a couple months longer than you."

Chuẩn asked,

"Did you come to Maine with your family?"

I replied,

"I am not married, my parents and my brothers are still in Vietnam. I am here by myself. Are you married?"

Chuẩn replied,

"Yes, I have a wife back home. We have no children."

I asked,

"How about the others, are they married, too?"

Chiêm Khén answered,

"I am married and have a little girl. Hiếu is also married, except Nguyên, he is still single."

78

Chiêm Khén complimented,

"You are brave."

I explained,

"Not really, sometimes you do what you have to do. It has nothing to do with bravery."

Nguyên expressed himself,

"You got guts coming to America by yourself. I do not think there are many single girls who could do what you are doing."

I said,

"Thank you for your confidence in me. Believe me I am trying harder than ever. Sometimes I shed tears on my pillows alone myself."

Chiêm Khén was touched by what I said and he comforted me saying,

"You have us now. You can share your problems with us."

I said,

"Thank you, I will remember that."

It was nine o'clock in the evening and dinner was ready. We sat together around the dining room table and ate our first dinner together in Limestone. We had beef stew over rice and mixed salad. Gus and the four Vietnamese complimented my cooking and asked me if I could show them my recipe. I had not told them about my first class restaurant nightclub business in Saigon that was successful until my departure. I did not want them to think that I was bragging about myself. At the end of the dinner I said,

"Well, it is getting late. I got to go now. I will see all of you tomorrow evening after five o'clock."

Chiêm Khén anxiously asked,

"Can you come earlier?"

I responded,

"I do not get off until five o'clock in the afternoon. So I will be here probably at five thirty or the latest at six o'clock, okay?"

Gus said,

"Let me take you to Loring Air Force Base, April. Your car is in the parking lot of the Education Center. You left it there this afternoon."

Loring Air Force Base was between Caribou and Limestone. Both were about the same distance. I had to leave my car there to meet Gus earlier.

During that period, I received a couple of letters from a young married Vietnamese lady, who had married a Marine Corp Captain. She worked for me in Vietnam when I was a manager at the CRA Club. She was one of my cashiers. When she was leaving her job at CRA, due to a reduction in our work force, I informed the Marine Second Lieutenant (he was a Lieutenant at that time in Saigon), who was a security police for the American Embassy, that she was leaving and I knew he would very much like to know. So I helped arrange him to meet her and shortly after this they married. After arriving in the United States, my ex-cashier friend wrote me several letters and asked me to help her younger sister and younger brother to leave for the States. They said they would reimburse me the expense money that I advanced and I was successful in helping them depart for the United States. What made it worse was that they never talked to me about their debt. She asked me if I could help her younger sister's boyfriend, who was also a new arrival refugee from Vietnam. She seemed anxious to get him out of their home in South Carolina. The reasons she gave me was that he could not find a job and at that time he had not yet married her sister. Thus, he was not a family member. Since I had previously met the young man in Guam four months earlier when he impressed me highly, and I agreed to accept him and do what I could with him there in Maine. Even though I found it extremely difficult to make it myself, I felt he was worthy of any help I could extend to him.

That evening, while in the middle of eating my supper, I received a phone call from South Carolina concerning the arrival of the young man. I picked up the phone and said,

"Hello."

At the other end the voice said,

"I am Rick calling from South Carolina. I received your letter today with your phone number. Therefore I am calling you up to talk with you about my coming to Maine to join you. It was nice meeting you in Guam even though it was only a couple hours. But you have made a great impression on me."

I replied,

"I enjoyed meeting you in Guam. I will help you here in Maine as best I can. Can you afford the airplane ticket to come to Maine?"

Rick said,

"I did quite a bit of yard work at the Marine Base and have enough for the ticket. I would just like to leave here. Lynn and Billy told me that I am not allowed to stay on the Marine Base because I am not a relative of their family."

I knew they lied to Rick. Lynn and Billy did not want him. So they had to make up a story. I asked him,

"What about your relationship with your girl friend, Kimberly? Do you really want to leave South Carolina without her?"

Rick explained,

"Kimberly is running around with a young Marine guy here named Johnny. They seem to get along very well. So I believe she and I are through. I do not have any reason to stay."

I said,

"Alright, just buy the ticket and inform me of your flight number and time of arrival. I will pick you up at the airport."

At the end of the week, Rick arrived at the Presque Isle airport. Mr. McDonald, the Dean of Presque Isle College, went to the airport to pick him up for me because I had a test with my class that afternoon. Mr. McDonald's wife and I were good friends. I ate dinner at their home every now and then.

Rick stayed around Mr. McDonald's office until I got out of my class. At the end of the day I drove Rick home with me. I asked him,

"Are you hungry?"

Rick answered,

"I ate on the airplane not too long ago. I am not hungry now. Are the people in this town friendly?"

How could I tell Rick about my very bad experience with Madeline and Sam? After all, it was not the town that treated me badly. It was just the opposite — they were super nice to me, so I replied,

"People here are good so do not worry. Now you have me and I have you. We will take care of one another. I know there is a Chinese Restaurant in town. You can go there and ask for a job, maybe as a dishwasher. Now you are only seventeen years old and by the time you are twenty you might become a chef at the restaurant and you might triple your salary."

I brought Rick to meet the four Vietnamese at Captain Blackwell's home. We became friends but Rick was always carrying a book and practiced his English, even when visiting with the Captain and the four refugees.

One weekend, Mr. Benfield invited me to his kitchen to taste his special made fudge that he baked from the oven. I brought Rick along and introduced him to Mr. Benfield, I said,

"Mr. Benfield, this is Rick, my younger stepbrother who is staying here with me. Is that alright with you?"

Mr. Benfield was about thirty eight years old. He was sincere. He smiled and said,

"That is okay, welcome to Maine. I want you and your stepsister to try my fudge. I love to make my own fudge on weekends, because my son, Brian and I love this recipe."

Mr. Benfield turned to Brian and said,

"Brian, say hello to April and her younger step brother."

Brian said,

"Hi, how are you?"

I replied,

"Hello Brian. We are fine."

I explained to Mr. Benfield about my assistance to Gus with the four Vietnamese refugees. After listening to me, Mr. Benfield said,

"He was a murderer. When the captain sat behind the controls of his B-52, people do not realize how easy it was for him to push the button and drop bombs on the North Vietnamese. He was no better or worse than anyone else. His guilty conscience bothered him to point that he must help somebody to release that bad feeling. If he really felt sorry for the Vietnamese, then why did he fly to Vietnam and bomb the people there?"

I defended the captain and said,

"He was doing his duty. He would be court-martialed if he did not do what he was told."

Mr. Benfield persisted,

"If I were him, I would have resigned from the Air Force and go to Canada for political asylum, and I would return back to the U. S. with a false identity. I could not kill and destroy thousand of lives like he did."

Rick was quiet for awhile. Suddenly he jointed Mr. Benfield and said,

"He was a Banana Pilot!"

(From the Vietnamese standpoint, pilots that took part in the bombing were called Banana Pilots, which was a derogatory term meaning 'going crazy.')

My younger stepbrother was very out spoken. He made a simple comment about the Captain's job and revealed to me that he also disagreed with the massive bombing of North Vietnam.

I explained

"It was the United States Air Force's job in Vietnam to bomb the North Vietnam enemy military targets. They did that for many years. Gus was no better or worse then anyone else. He just blindly followed orders like all other military personnel all over the world since the beginning of time. I am not a hero worshiper. I am speaking from my own point of view."

To change the most unpleasant subject, I put my arms around little Brian and said,

"Let us go and swing in the back yard. You sit in the swing and I will push you, okay"

Mr. Benfield smiled and kidded with us,

"If you wait until Brian is a grown up man, he will marry you, April."

Little Brian picked up a couple pieces of fudge and then ran out to the back yard. I followed after him. I said to Rick,

"You can come with us. Mr. Benfield, I will catch you later. I am going to play with Brian in the back yard."

VI

Meeting in Arlington

Gus appeared by the door in my office, at noon, at the Education Center. I greeted him with a smile and said.

"Hi Gus, come on in. What can I do for you?"

Gus came in my office and before he said anything, he leaned over and kissed me on my lips. In a few seconds, I raised my finger and signaled Gus. I said,

"Just a second Gus. What are you doing? Do you think I am some kind of Suzie Wong in a bar in Hong Kong?"

I stepped over to the door and on the outside hung the clock sign stating, 'Will return at one o'clock'. I closed and locked the door. I then put my arms around Gus's large shoulders and Gus said,

"I miss doing this with you. I just want to be left alone with you for a few moments."

I said,

"You are right. We have been so busy with others. We have never been alone together."

Gus kissed me tenderly; I then felt his hand move down to my hips and pulled my body closer to him. I put my hand on his hand and said,

"I am hungry! Are you taking me to lunch?"

Gus said,

"Should we go to the officers club near here?"

I answered,

"Why not? Let me get my purse and comb my hair. You are a dare devil. You messed it up with your inquisitive fingers."

When we arrived at the officer's club, Gus had me pick a table near the window. We sat down and the waiter arrived at the table with a menu. Gus ordered orange juice and broiled cod and I ordered cold cuts and club soda. Gus looked at me and said,

"Christmas is coming and I am thinking of taking you and the guys to see my mother in Greensboro, North Carolina for the Holidays. What do you think about that?"

I answered,

"I have no plans for this Christmas. I could go to Greensboro with you and the guys."

Gus said,

"We will leave Maine on the twenty-second because it is quite a ways from here to North Carolina. My mother lives there with my two younger brothers who are still in college. My mother is divorced and she owns a clothing store in Greensboro. She is fifty-two years old and still in good health. She will be glad to see you. The other evening I phoned her and she said she is looking forward to meeting you and the guys."

I then asked Gus,

"Are you sure you want to do that?"

Gus answered,

"Definitely! On the way we will stop to see my uncle in Arlington, Virginia next to Washington D.C."

I paused for a moment and said,

"I know a couple people in Washington D.C. Maybe I could see them while we are in that area. Do you mind?"

Gus inquired,

"Who do you want to see?"

I answered,

"They are old friends I knew back home. One is a lawyer and the other is a business woman. I would like to call them when we get there at your uncles home."

After lunch, Gus took me back to my office and as he left he said,

"Today is the tenth of December. We have two weeks to get ready for the trip. Call me if you need me."

Christmas of 1975 came. Only Chuẩn and Nguyên came along with Gus and rode to Greensboro, North Carolina. The other two, Chiêm Khén and Hiếu, remained in Limestone to spend Christmas with their girlfriends whom they had met while harvesting potatoes in the fields. The girls were eighteen and nineteen years old and were granddaughters of a rich farmer in the area. They came over to keep the guys company from time to time and sometimes we all went out dancing at the local night club. Captain Mike Homer, Gus's friend, was twenty-seven years old. He was tall and well built. He always came around my younger stepbrother to give him moral support or to take him different places. Mike got along well with the four Vietnamese young men. Mike had a mother and older brother who lived in Smithfield, North Carolina. He was also going home for Christmas to see his mother and brother. Mike decided to ride with Rick in his car and we were to meet in Greensboro.

Driving from Caribou to Arlington, Virginia was quite a distance. The Captain drove all the way to New York City in his 1973 Pontiac Lemans. When we were about to enter New York City area, Gus gave me the wheel so he could sleep for awhile.

Every one of us respected Gus, not only because he was a captain, but also a fine young, handsome man. When he smiled, he had a pretty dimple on his cheek and this made him very cute. I took over the driving and proceeded. I had never been in New York City before and never drove in heavy traffic like New York. I was very confused with all the street signs along the expressway. When I thought of the four people in the car including myself, my sense of responsibility came to my head and I kept proceeding.

We arrived at Arlington, Virginia about six o'clock in the evening and met Gus's Uncle. He was the president of the National Virginia Bank. He was in his early forties, married and had two small daughters, aged six and four years old. He had a five-bedroom house with a large swimming pool in the back yard. Gus's uncle, Carl, was a fine person, friendly and soft spoken. His wife was the daughter of the Consul of the Turkish Embassy in Washington D.C. He and his wife greeted us warmly and he said,

"Hello. Welcome to our home. Please come in. You all must have had a long drive here. Just relax and we will have dinner together."

Carl's wife, Diana said,

"I do not cook. We usually eat out or T.V. dinners. Our kids are easily fed. They do not argue with me about what I feed them. Gus's uncle is also not fussy. When he gets home, he goes to the kitchen himself and fixes his own dinner. I have two kids to take care of, so there is no time for me to do anything else."

I do not understand why American wives do not take charge of household matters, while the men are out earning a living. However, I said,

"I can cook, and I will cook dinner for everybody. But I have a couple of people I know in Washington, D.C. that I want to call. Can I use your phone Carl?"

Carl replied,

"Help yourself and feel at home. I will have to go for an hour to take care of some business. I will be back by the time we eat dinner, okay?"

I told Chuẩn and Nguyên, that the wife of the bank president does not cook. She only knows how to make babies.

Chuẩn joked,

"Ah, she is a lazy sergeant (meaning Diana, who does not cook for the family). If she does not cook, she should be demoted to a corporal or serve ten days in the stockade."

Nguyên jointed in commenting,

"If the sergeant does not cook, then she needs to be in the frontier of the battle field."

I declared,

"The bank president loves her. So you guys be quiet. She is a nice person. Besides, cooking is not mandatory for a woman in America."

Carl left the house shortly thereafter. Diana told me to make myself at home. I then asked Chuẩn and Nguyên to help me get the meat out of the freezer and clean up the vegetables so I would have time to make a phone call to Washington D.C. Gus told me that after dinner, he was going to a party where his old school friends and neighbors would all attend. His mother and father had divorced years before in Washington D.C. But some of his old friends were still there. I said,

"Good, I have a couple friends who I have not seen in a good while. I want to see them while I am in Arlington."

Gus appeared to be jealous that I did not understand. He was going to attend a party that evening by himself. Why was he jealous of me going out to see my old friends? Gus said,

"Be good, and do not stay out too late."

I really did not like Gus's resentful attitude. He had a party to go to and have fun with his old friends and had not invited any of us. Why should he worry about me going out with my old friends? Besides, these friends of mine could help me with my future in the United States. They were a lawyer and businesswoman in the country. By seeing them, it might do us some good. So, I said,

"Do not worry about me. Just go out and have a good time."

I liked what Gus did for the four young Vietnamese, but other than that he upset me. He was a typical military professional and self-centered. I continued,

"I will never ever marry a military man, Gus. Most of you are like robots and military means violence."

I did not realize it but my words, I believed, influenced Gus to quit the Air Force later.

VII

Brief Relation

I dialed the phone number and when they picked up, I asked

"Is this Mrs. White's resident?"

The voice answered,

"Yes this is Mrs. White."

I said,

"Mrs. White, my name is April Nguyên. Your son, Big John, gave me this number before leaving Saigon for the United States. I am now in Arlington, Virginia. Is Big John in?"

Mrs. White replied,

"Oh, April I have heard so much about you from Big John. He is now in Crystal City. He bought a condominium with two bedrooms. Let me give you his phone number. By the way, if you have the time, drop in and see me in Washington D.C. Here is his number, 202-644-3112."

She gave me his number. I said,

"Thank you Mrs. White. I will stop by and see you sometime later. Goodbye."

I then phoned Big John and when someone picked up I said, "Is John White there?"

They answered,

"This is he."

I said,

"Big John, this is April. I am now in Arlington, Virginia. How are you?"

Big John said joyfully,

"Ah! April. It has been so long since I heard from you the last time. Can I come and pick you up to show you where I live. I am about forty-five minutes from Arlington."

By this time Carl walked in. I asked Carl to give Big John the directions to get to his house.

At nine o'clock in the evening, Big John showed up. I introduced Big John to Carl, and I said,

"This is John White, a lawyer in the United States whom I had met back in Saigon."

Carl shook hands with Big John and then Big John and I left the house shortly.

Big John and I arrived at his home at ten forty-five in the evening. We talked about the good old friends including André in old Saigon. Big John was interested in knowing what I wanted to do and where I wanted to live. In actuality, Big John wished for me to relocate at Washington D.C. I asked Big John if he could pick me up tomorrow. I told him that I needed to see an old girlfriend while in Washington D.C.

Big John arrived at Uncle Blackwell's home in Arlington at ten o'clock in the morning the next day. He had on a sport coat and tie. I was up earlier that morning while everybody else in the house was asleep. It was the weekend and many people did not like to get up early except me. Big John said,

"How are you this morning? You look mighty well."

I said,

"Thank you. But you can not judge a book by its cover. I am ready to go Big John?"

On our way to his car, which was parked two blocks from Carl's home, Big John explained to me the many ways he was needed in Saigon. He said,

"I am a lawyer from the United States. I was also an advisor to the Military Air Command Vietnam (M.A.C.V.) to keep everybody's nose clean, and a religious connector of the Buddhist Sectors in Saigon. I love South Vietnam and I hope I made some good contributions to the people there. April, you see, I was not there for any devious reason!"

I loved Big John. He was a very good lawyer. While in Saigon, Big John helped to arrange some important meetings between Buddhist monks and the commander-in-chief of the

M.A.C.V. Buddhism is the major religion in South Vietnam. Sometimes the government's decisions had to follow the monk's approval. They are the messengers of our God. They say prayers for the sake of peace in South Vietnam. Big John also studied the proposals of the M.A.C.V. commanders and relayed this to Buddhist leaders to get them into action. I looked at Big John and said,

"I am not here to judge you or anyone of my friends. I am here to enjoy a visit with you my friend. How about getting something to eat, quickly?"

Big John joked,

"How about eating some crackers with French mustard?"

Big John reminded me that while in Saigon, he ate like a vegetarian. Everything was non-fattening, and the Buddhist monks liked him very well. Big John insisted on going to a restaurant that required wearing a coat and tie. I suggested that we go to Kentucky Fried Chicken. It is fast and the food is delicious. Big John asked,

"April, when did you start liking fried chicken?"

(He was implying that I was a "chicken" to leave Vietnam.)

I replied to him without hesitation,

"The minute I became a "chicken" in the United States, I liked chicken. That is why you and I get along so well." I thought to myself that he is no different from me. He was in a hurry to leave Vietnam just as I was. We were both afraid about the idea.

Big John scolded me in a loving manner,

"April, you used sarcasm."

I said,

"Well Big John, are we going to get something to eat? I am starving, my friend."

We left the restaurant and headed to Big John's mothers home. Big John introduced me to his mother. She lived in a three-bedroom condo located in downtown Washington D.C. Big John was the only child. His mother lived alone since her husband passed away some years before. Mrs. White was a very generous person. I saw her slip a fifty dollar bill in her butler's pocket. From talking to Big John later, I understood that she tipped him on a regular basis. Mrs. White greeted me with a smile and said,

"Please sit down and make yourself comfortable. Would you like a shot of French cognac?"

Since Mrs. White was going to have a shot of cognac herself, I said,

"Yes, thank you."

Mrs. White began,

"I have heard that you are quite a lady. Big John has told me of your achievements in helping the unfortunate people in Saigon. I worried so much about John while he was there. Thank God, he is home at last."

I knew how a mother was concerned about the safety of her son.

I said,

"Big John used to live in one of the most secured areas. No terrorists or guerrillas were able to penetrate within, and no rockets could be targeted. He lived in a very expensive home area in town. There were happy parties only and no war or fighting at all."

At this point Mrs. White got out of her chair and went to her desk at the other side of her living room and said,

"April, I wrote you a check for some personal shopping. You need a few things for yourself. I will write you a check soon. This is just a token, please accept it. I wish you all the best, and drop in to see me when you are in town."

We said goodbye to Mrs. White and headed to the East side of Washington D.C. to see my girlfriend. Big John said,

"My mother is impressed with you and likes you very much. I hope you will relocate to Washington D.C."

I replied,

"Maybe later, Big John. I have so much in my mind about what to do after my visit here in Washington D.C. Anyhow, I will keep you informed."

I rang the doorbell at her apartment and in a couple moments, Sister Heidi was at the door to greet me, and said,

"Come on in, April. How is everything? Is your family alright?" (In the oriental culture, people refer to a close friend as a brother and sister.)

I said,

"They are alright and everything is fine. Sister Heidi, I would like you to meet John White, a lawyer friend of mine from Washington D.C. But we just call him Big John. You can totally trust us. We are here only for the purpose of visiting you."

Sister Heidi wrapped my hands in hers and said, "It is very good to see you."

I said in a lower voice so no one could hear us,

"The last two million liters of gasoline you handed over to me, I had to dump it on a fat-ass Chinese merchant, who owned the large gas station outside of the city limits."

Sister Heidi assured me,

"I knew that Chinese guy. He was fat and stunk like gasoline, but his money was worth a thousand gold bars. When we had the business and could not handle it, he always came to our rescue. He was willing to store a million liters of gasoline!"

Sister Heidi continued,

"The Hawaiian-American left the American Embassy in Saigon for Hawaii. After he handed us the last two million liters of gasoline, take a guess how much money he made in five years? It must be a great deal of money."

I said,

"Since the war in Vietnam came close to an end, corruption existed at every level in Saigon. If that Hawaiian-American did not do it, somebody else would have done the same, and I think the courts in America would run out of room with all the corrupt people. Can we blame them? In Saigon, many making a living were crooked with the black market in some way. Only the poor folks in the country were innocent."

I continued,

"The two million litters of gasoline almost got my girlfriend in trouble with the local Vietnamese authorities as a part of the group. Our competitor offered a nickel less per liter. So that is it. We were stuck with two million liters of gasoline, and I did not get any from our last deal. How about some spare gasoline so I could drive across the country?"

Sister Heidi responded,

"Oh, that is easy: I will be more than happy to go to the bank with you. Is three thousand dollars enough?" She gave me this to keep me quiet. I told no one, but I have written about it.

I replied,

"I greatly appreciate your generosity and consideration. May God bless you."

The three of us left Sister Heidi's apartment to go to the bank that afternoon. I had accomplished a big deal during my visit to Washington D.C. How lucky I was to have had some success to help ease the pain as a new arrival in the United States.

Big John dropped me off at Carl's home. He asked,

"April, are you sure that you want to leave?"

I said,

"Yes, Big John. I am not a very happy person now. I will call upon you when I am lonesome. I will think of you as my very wonderful friend. Give my love to your mother and thank you."

Big John never used rough or profane language in my presence. He was kind and gentle with me at all times.

VIII

Arrival at Greensboro

We arrived at Gus's mother's home in Greensboro just in time to celebrate Christmas Eve in 1975. I volunteered to do the cooking. In the kitchen, I suddenly heard Gus's voice from behind,

"You are seductive, April. Watch out for my younger brothers and their friends. They will be out to get you."

I blushed and defended myself,

"You are not innocent and you are the one that I have to watch out for. I am not here to play around with anybody, no matter what."

Gus was standing close enough so that as soon as I turned around to confront him, he wrapped his arms around me while both of his hands grasped my butt and pulled me closer to him. Why did this man like my butt all the time? We had intimate

112

relationships in discretion so the Vietnamese guys would not be jealous of Gus.

At the dining table of the family there was Gus, his mother, Keith and Paul (Gus's younger brothers), Chuẩn, Nguyên, an artistic lady, a local journalist, and myself. Gus explained,

"The United States of America believes in freedom. We will fight anyone to keep freedom alive. Just as during the war, our purpose was to save South Vietnam for freedom and to abolish communism."

Gus looked at me and said,

"April, the cost of the flight practice for the U.S. Air Force was so high. It could feed the whole Vietnam, North and South for many decades to come."

I needed to support my captain friend who was quite intelligent. In his statement he revealed the many reasons for supporting the South Vietnamese government and the use of B-52's. I then replied to Gus,

"Your belief is not so different from many of us. The South Vietnamese also loved their freedom. That is why we fought the war for our beliefs.

IX

The Cold Winter

As time went by, my boss, Mr. McDonald, and I had to move our office to the Presque Isle location, in the Northern Maine Vocational Technical Institute. I had to drive twenty-four miles one way from Caribou every work day. Also, I was a full-time student at the school studying business.

Hard times had passed and life in Maine was peaceful for a while. I returned the car I borrowed from Mr. Forsyth. I offered him a dollar a day for the use of his car. I had purchased a used car, a 1969 Ford LTD. It had become a close friend to me as it was my only way of getting around. I was able to go to school and work because of the LTD. One of the reasons I bought a big car was to drive to Atlanta with all my luggages. It allowed me room to carry a great deal with me. I had twelve suitcases, which I brought from Saigon. André was good enough to send me the rest of my twelve suitcases from his home in Bloomington, Illinois. My younger stepbrother commented,

"Sister April, you need a train to carry all your belongings."

I answered,

"Do not worry about it. This big Ford LTD will handle all of it. Otherwise, I would have purchased a smaller car, which does not burn a lot of gas."

Rick got along with me very well. He was always cordial. He was respectful of any comment or decision I made to facilitate our goals or achievements. We went to the Calvary Baptist Church in Caribou every Sunday. There we met the Richardson family consisting of five: Darrel, Wilma, Cindy, Robert and Denise. Darrell was a deacon at the church and a major with the Air Force. We became good friends with the Richardsons.

By going to the Mormon Church with me, Rick met Janice and her parents. Janice's father was a retired captain also from the Air Force. They were Mormons. Rick and I visited there and that is how he met her.

Rick had been going to high school at Caribou for three months. He made straight A's in math but failed English. He came home from school one day and said,

"My math was good but English is terrible. I need to study much more so I can go to college."

I asked,

"What do you want to do when you get through college?"

Rick replied,

"I want to be an automobile factory engineer."

I asked,

"Do you want to build a car? There are so many engineers in the States. How would you be able to compete with them?"

Rick replied,

"I would build cars that burn less gasoline, that have lighter bodies and a more durable engine. In this way, the new car would be economical for everyone to own."

I inquired,

"Have you met girls your age at school?"

Rick said,

"There is a girl in my class whom I always admire. She has a very pretty face. Today the teacher called her to his desk and she had a skirt on which showed her skinny legs like the two straight pipes going all the way up to her hips. So that is the end of my saga about girls."

I asked,

"What about Janice, who you met at her church? She is pretty and she is from a nice family. Don't you think?"

Rick said,

"Yes, but she is a Mormon. She does not drink tea, coffee or beer, and there are many restrictions in her religion. I do not think it would work out."

I suggested,

"If you are not going to marry anyone, why not make friends and keep them company to go to movies or restaurants on your day off."

Rick asked,

"How do I get to her house at the top of the hill in Presque Isle on a cold winter day like this?"

I said,

"Do you know how to drive a car back home?"

Rick answered,

"I know how to drive but I do not have a driver's license."

I said,

"That is not okay, but you can drive once in awhile and I trust you will stay out of trouble for me. We go against the law by you driving the car without a driver's license. But we are in a small town and hopefully the law enforcement is not too strict like in New York."

Rick asked,

"So can I have the car this afternoon? I promise to drive the car very carefully and take good care of it."

I said,

"Yes you can have the car, but promise me that you will be a gentleman with her and treat her well. I want to rest at home this afternoon. You surprised me about your thoughts of what you want to be. That is okay, a dream never hurts."

Rick modestly said,

"Sister, I am planning to go to college but how do I pay the school tuition. I have got to work to support myself. Lynn and Billy, the couple in South Carolina, told me to join the Army or Navy because I could receive the GI Bill to pay for my school. I respect your opinion; can you tell me what I should do?"

I explained,

"We are from a war torn country. Now we are in another country. Why do you want to go into the Military Armed Forces? Why do you want to go to war? There is a way for you to go to college through a government grant or loan. On Monday, when I go to school, I will check this out with my boss and I will let you know."

Rick went to the closet and put his heavy winter coat on. Before he walked to the car, he told me to take care of myself, I said,

"Winter in Maine is so rough. I feel depressed most of the time. But that is normal, do not worry about me. Just drive very carefully on the road. One of these days everyone will have to get out and do things for themselves. You might as well start doing that now."

I wanted him to become independent. I saw tears in his eyes as he was walking to the car. I must not be weak for his sake. He just turned eighteen and he would have to learn to be on his own soon. Maybe then he could help me, if I ever needed it.

Janice's parents lived on top of a hill in Presque Isle. It is about one and half miles from the main street to the top of the hill. I had been invited to eat dinner at her family's home once before so I knew about the distance to her home. On the way down, Rick slid the car into a snow bank. After digging in the snow, he still could not get the car out. He then called up a

121

friend he knew in Presque Isle to come with his truck to pull the car out. Instead of pulling the car out, they tore the rear bumper off. He was upset and called me from Presque Isle. He said,

"Sister, the car is in a snow bank and I cannot get it out. Maybe we will get it out tomorrow morning because the snow is falling down heavily in Presque Isle. A friend of mine here came out to help me and we tore off the rear bumper of your car. He can take me home. I am very sorry."

I was not upset but worried about how would I get to school and work in the morning. I said,

"Come on home and do not worry. I will call a tow truck in the morning. Tell your friend to drive very carefully."

An hour later, Rick arrived home. His hair was wet and his coat covered with snow. He was upset and said,

"I am very sorry, sister. I did not mean to leave the car there. But you told me to come on home."

I comforted him with,

"We will worry about it tomorrow. It was not your fault, but the weather condition was bad. Have you eaten yet? Look in the refrigerator to see if there is anything you can eat. I was not very concerned about the car, but for your safety and I am glad to see that you are alright."

Four days later I sent Rick to J.C. Penny's Department Store in Caribou. My younger stepbrother, an inexperienced driver, drove the car into the J.C. Penny's building causing further damage. The right front end of the car was crushed in like it was in dire need of a nose job. I had no money to fix it so I just drove the way it was — beat up!

As winter set in, the clothes that we thought would be warm enough, were not. I took my meager savings and bought winter clothes for Rick and me. Due to the extreme weather, I developed various illnesses and all my savings dwindled for doctor bills. I was so sick my younger stepbrother was in tears. He shook his coin bank to get some money to go to the market and buy some oranges so I could eat to strengthen me.

X

Under Suspicion

On a Saturday night Gus and the four refugees and I got together and I cooked. The guys helped by cleaning the house and chopped wood for the cold winter. They also helped in the kitchen. Gus asked me to sit down at the dinning table and with tears in his eyes, he said,

"I bombed the VC to help the South Vietnamese keep their land. I could not see all the VC guerillas terrorizing the South. I could not stand the thought of the South Vietnamese living with great terror from the VC. My plane could have been shot down like some of my colleagues were. But I wanted to help stop the invasion of the VC on South Vietnam."

I got up to stir the soup. Everybody had a beer that night.

In the living room another captain by the name of Mike Homer and co-pilot Leroy Burger, were also at the party. My best girl friend, Judy Cameron, whom I met at the memorial hospital in Caribou, was a nurse at the hospital. Judy was twenty-three years old, heavy set but cute. Judy always admired Gus for his military rank and handsome looks. She told me that Gus was a big shot in Limestone because there were not many captains in her town. Judy lived with her grandmother whose home was in the neighborhood of Gus' home in Limestone. Tonight Judy had a few beers and told me that she liked Gus very much and she wanted to get to know him better. Judy said,

"Hey April, I think Gus likes me. He asked me to come over to his house earlier today to help him hang up the blinds on the windows in his living room."

I said,

"Judy, my friend, do not depend on your imagination too much. When you know for sure that Gus really likes you, tell me about that. Most military men like to travel and they do not like just one girl."

Judy inquired,

"Have you done anything with him?"

I said,

"That is not your concern. I just do not want to mix up my friendship with you and Gus. I like you a lot and I want to keep it that way for a long time. Maybe some day you will understand how much I like you." (I assumed that young Judy was a virgin. Gus just wanted to play around.)

Judy hugged me for a couple seconds and then returned to Rick and the four Vietnamese. I still had not recovered from my illness, but in spite of this I went to Gus' home that night to insure good communication between the Captain and his fellow refugees. When Gus carried the wood from the garage to the fireplace located in the living room, he passed where I was working preparing the food. He gave me a kiss on my lips. Unfortunately, Chiêm Khén and Nguyên saw this through the window. Later they told me that their sponsor was in love with me. As Nguyên and Chiêm Khén continued to help Gus carry wood, Nguyên said,

"April, the Captain likes you."

I denied,

"I do not think so, Nguyên."

Nguyên continued,

"We saw Gus kiss you from the window."

I blamed it on Gus so that I could stay neutral with the guys. I said,

"I have no control over his actions, especially when he approaches me from behind."

In the orient, men are the masters and they are the ones to make the first move towards a woman. All possible approaches by a man for a good relationship with a woman are more common in the oriental society. Women that are too aggressive are not well regarded in the eyes of the majority of men. Traditionally, Vietnamese women are supposed to be submissive to men. Therefore, when the four young

Vietnamese men told me about what they saw, I felt that my answers to them would get their sympathy for me as a submissive traditional Vietnamese woman and then it would be more acceptable for Gus to kiss me.

Nguyên and Chiêm Khén walked into the living room and dropped the firewood down. I followed in behind them. I had a beer in my hand. I was not feeling well. I was still sick from the severe winter in Maine. I felt nauseated and Gus saw me getting pale. But he did not realize how sick I had been for the past couple of days. He joked,

"April, do not throw up on the floor. I will throw you out on the porch."

I had only been in the States a relatively short while and I did not understand that Americans joke around like that. I took what the Captain said as an insult. I had worked very hard all day and then worked hard in the kitchen of this house. I also had picked up the refugees earlier at five in the morning and had given them a ride home in the evening. So when Gus made the comment about my sick condition, it made me angry also causing the refugee's anger at Gus. I had not been in the United States long enough to realize that people joke like that.

Chiêm Khén was older than the other three Vietnamese. He asked me to tell him what his sponsor said. After I told him what Gus said, he then said,

"April, do you want me to hit him. Just tell me yes or no if you do not like his joke."

Rick heard all this, and then said to Chiêm Khén,

"Sister April has been ill for days. But your 'Banana' captain does not know about that. He thought April was sick because of drinking beer."

Rick's response only made matters worse.

Chiêm Khén said,

"Why did not you say something and why did you conceal your illness?"

I explained,

"If I could not help myself, how could I help you? I did not want to worry any of you. You have enough problems in adjusting in your new country yourselves. Why should I worry you?"

Chiêm Khén and the other Vietnamese told Gus what happened to me. They urged me to lay down in one of the bedrooms upstairs. But I insisted on remaining in the living room until the party was over. When I was in the driveway ready to drive home, my car would not move because of the pile of snow underneath. Gus came out with a shovel to dig the snow out from the rear tires. Soon Rick and I were on our way home that night. The distance from Limestone to Caribou was fourteen miles and snow was everywhere — deep snow! Since it was one o'clock in the morning and the road was empty, I drove in the middle of the road towards Caribou for a couple miles. I was suddenly stopped by the local Police Patrol. He signaled me to stop my car. He walked to my car and asked me to roll my car window down. He asked me,

"Are you drunk, ma'am?"

I answered,

"No sir."

The policeman asked,

"Why did you drive the car in a middle of the road?"

I explained,

"I am an interpreter for Gus and four Vietnamese refugees in Limestone. They had a party earlier but I did not drink. I drove the car in middle of the road because there was too much snow on the road. It covers the road so I was afraid to drive the car into the ditch and it is late at night. I did not want to get stuck in the middle of this cold winter. So I drove in middle of the road for safety."

The policeman said,

"I know Gus. Since your breath does not smell alcohol you can go but drive on the right side of the road, ma'am. Thanks and have a safe trip."

Gus was a well educated man. He was twenty-six when I met him. He joined the Air Force when he was nineteen years old. Perhaps, during seven years in the service, Gus acquired a military attitude and became somewhat like a robot. I think it went so far that he trivialized his fate. How could he joke about the state of my health? The four Vietnamese theorized that Gus had consumed some beer and lost his sense of joking and good taste. They were attached to me. But from my outlook, my relationship with them was totally platonic. Gus appeared jealous of their protective position. Since the four Vietnamese did not understand English, I concealed my feelings and told them that the Captain merely used poor judgment in joking about my health.

After a couple of days I felt much better. I met Gus at the Education Center and I told him,

"I am writing a book."

Gus responded,

"You are writing a book? Maybe Playboy Magazine will publish your book in their magazine."

He joked about the idea of my writing a book. His kidding upset me. I was hoping he would help me in writing my book. But he made fun of my idea. So I said,

"You may be right. I would be lucky to have Playboy Magazine publish my book. Just think Gus, if I am successful, I could buy you a couple of drinks."

Gus chuckled,

"For sure, and I will buy the magazine too."

Gus continued,

"You remind me of a book about Suzzie Wong, who was a bargirl in Hong Kong. She was so beautiful that she melted all the hearts of American GIs on the island."

I said,

"Suzzie Wong was a bargirl and fraternized with the American GI's in Hong Kong. How could you compare me with a prostitute?"

Gus said in an apologetic manner as he held my hand in his,

"Alright, Miss April. I am sorry to refer to you as a bargirl who is overly sexed. I wanted to say that you have the same look of beautiful Suzzie Wong. If I offended you, I apologize."

I over looked that idiot Gus, but I was very angry with his stupid comment.

Gus said,

"I know a girl at Loring Air Force Base named Loretta. She is eighteen years old and the daughter of my boss, Colonel Edmond Humphrey. She is attending college at Durham, North Carolina."

"When did you meet her?" I asked.

"About one week after meeting you. She asked me to go to Durham to see her on New Year's Day." Gus said.

I asked Gus,

"Are you going?"

"I do not know. If I go to see her, maybe she could talk to her father, whom is my boss, to approve my transfer request to another city. I wish I did not have to go, April." Gus answered.

134

I did not like Gus's manner so I said,

"You are a grown up man. You should know what you want to do. I can not tell you what to do. If you have to help your career, that is your choice. But if you want to have fun with her, that is another matter. I do not want to influence you one way or another. If you asked me, I would say no. But ultimately, it is up to you."

Gus said,

"I will leave Limestone on the thirtieth and will be back on the second. We will go to the Air Force promotion party for all officers at the base. Will you go with me?"

"Sure, I will see you when you get back. Have fun." I replied.

Gus was really a butterfly. He was not as serious a man as I thought. He wanted to play around and have a good time just like I had explained to Judy. How could he play a game where he would not win? He will not win Loretta's heart or mine. Loretta was aware through outside sources, that Gus was not available.

On the second, Gus returned to Limestone, Maine. As agreed, Gus took me to the Air Force promotion party for the officers at Loring Air Force Base. I looked my best that evening. All the Air Force officers were in black tuxedos and the wives were gorgeous in their evening gowns. Gus was always by my side. He said,

"You are a princess tonight, and I am proud of you. I missed you."

"Thank you. I just wish that the cold winter was over soon so I could get all my gear together and leave this area. Did you have a good time in Durham?" I said sternly.

Gus believed he was clever. But he was sadly mistaken because I saw through his little game. He said,

"Loretta dragged me down to her bed."

The slight affection I had for Gus melted away at that moment. The tie that bound us was my concern for the four young Vietnamese men that Gus sponsored. I answered,

"Butterflies have all the fun. They live the hardest because they only live for a short time. In this case, Gus only lives for whoring around."

At this point Gus felt like he was being belittled and he attempted to defend himself by saying,

"April, you are sharp and sophisticated in your statement. I spent much more money on the trip with you to Greensboro, North Carolina than the money I spent with Loretta. Can you see the difference?"

Gus worked on my sympathy but it did not convince me simply because I knew that his mind was going in one direction and his heart was going in the opposite direction.

At the end of the evening, Gus took me home and walked me into my apartment. Gus held me in his arms and said,

"Do you want me to stay for awhile?"

"No, you had better be going." I was very cool with my answer.

"You are stubborn, April."

Gus left the apartment disappointed and went to his car in the driveway.

A white blanket of snow covered the ground over the whole state of Maine. The temperature was thirty-two degrees below zero. The snow flakes were flying down from a quiet sky that night. I looked out the window and felt loneliness with the freezing white snow all around. I picked up the telephone and called Virginia.

A familiar voice on the other end said,

"This is Nathan speaking."

"It is me Nathan." I said.

Nathan's voice was exhilarated,

"April, you are found again. I thought I had lost you for sure. I asked André where you were but he only gave me some vague story. How about staying put long enough so I can see you and feel that it is really you. I want to see you — anywhere."

I was overwhelmed by Nathan's enthusiasm, I told him,

138

"Can you come to Maine? I have a small one bedroom apartment with my young stepbrother. He sleeps in the living room. I would share my bedroom with you. My stepbrother and I have some friends and I would like you to meet them."

When I called Nathan up, it was Tuesday night. Nathan immediately replied,

"I am going to book my reservation flight on Friday evening so I can stay a week with you, okay?"

"Okay Nathan, I will look forward to your arrival. I will meet you at the airport." I said.

As usual, I continued to meet Gus and the four young Vietnamese men at his home two or three times a week. This Wednesday afternoon I told Gus,

"An old friend of mine from Virginia is coming to see me in Caribou, Maine for a week. I will not be seeing you during that time."

Gus looked sad with a long face and disapprovingly he said,

"You make it sound like a contest when it should not be."

I responded,

"You made the contest, not me. However, we still stand as we are today or this can be what you make of our relationship."

My words made him realize what he had missed. The boat had left the seashore, and he missed the boat. I was out of his life already at that instant moment. Gus said,

"April, I am your boyfriend."

I said,

"It depends how I feel after Nathan's visit with me."

"April, I will talk to you later." Gus said.

I left Gus's house and headed back to Caribou.

The week of Nathan's visit in Maine was wonderful. We went over to Canada to dine in a popular French restaurant and drove around the Canadian countryside to see the beautiful mountains and lakes. We also went to the fairground in Canada, where there was the horse race with many tourists from United States. Nathan, I and my younger stepbrother bet on the race. For the first time in my life I gambled. I was excited

140

to see the horses run. We lost our bets but we had a great time together. Nathan was always around me and never failed to give me first class treatment. Three of my friends were Air Force captains and they were jealous with Nathan taking up all my time during that week. A girlfriend of mine, Judy, who was a nurse at the local hospital, was attracted to Nathan. Everyone loved Nathan.

At the end of the day, Nathan, my stepbrother and I took off from Canada back to Caribou, Maine. We dropped Rick, my stepbrother off at the apartment and then we went to a coffee shop near by. I lamented to Nathan,

"Nathan, there is something wrong. We can not be intimate, why?"

He said,

"Nothing's wrong my dear. I am just too amazed with getting together with you. You are like a mythology in a fairy-tale. I am in disbelief of this reunion."

I sadly said,

"Are you afraid of me or of my writing about you?"

(He knew, I was constantly writing about my experiences and I thought he felt I would write about him).

"Look, I have no guns. I can not hurt anybody. When we were in bed together, our lack of intimacy brought a problem up. You reacted to me as though I had held a gun to your head. I did all I could - what happened, Nathan?"

Nathan comforted me with,

"I do not know why, my dear. You are very attractive to me. Every time I look at you I want you. I can not explain my lack of virility in bed with you."

"I do not know Nathan. There' has got to be an answer to this problem. Anyhow, I am not feeling very good about my experience with you. I feel like there is something wrong with me. I do not want to talk about it now. Let us go home, Nathan." I said.

A couple days before Nathan left Maine, to fly back to Virginia, Rick and I took Nathan to see our friends, the four young Vietnamese refugees at Gus's home. When we arrived, an airman who was part of the same crew with Gus stated,

"Vietnamese women are so fragile. They let everything bother them."

Scott, the airman who was part of Gus's crew, probably had learned quickly about the break-up between Gus and me. Therefore, when he made the above statement, Nathan demonstrated his objection towards what Scott had said by brushing my shoulder off before their eyes and said,

"Not really. You do not know much about Vietnamese. So you should not make a hasty conclusion about people that you do not know."

Nathan was big, tall and determined, thus Gus and Scott (airman crew) did not argue back but quietly listened to Nathan's opinion. They did not know why I was so important to someone like Nathan. They only knew one thing, that I was a refugee from a war torn country.

Nathan flew back to Virginia. He wanted me to come down to Virginia to see him so he could show me the college and his home, where I might want to attend school.

The weekend came and Nathan sent me a round trip airplane ticket to Virginia. Nathan picked me up at the airport and brought me to his home. He lived fifty miles outside Washington D.C. His home was a two story condo and absolutely spotless. Nathan said,

"I had the house cleaned up just for you. Take a look around the house and tell me if you like it."

Nathan showed me his train model playroom, he said,

"I play the model train when I am by myself and it is really fun to run the train through the tunnels. Also, I like to paint the cars different colors. Every now and then, I rebuild the trains and the cars."

I asked,

"How much does it cost you for these trains?"

"Two grand. But I really enjoy this kind of a toy. Get the remote control and press the button and guess what, the train moves down the tracks."

I pressed the remote control and the whole train started from start to finish throughout the tunnels, hills and mountains and the train's whistle sounded like the real one.

I asked Nathan,

"Are we the only two that are going to dinner tonight?"

"No, we have a married couple who are my best friends and they are coming with us. Is that okay with you?" Nathan answered.

I said to Nathan,

"I need to change my clothes Nathan. Do you mind if I go in the bathroom to refresh myself?"

Nathan showed me to the bathroom on the second floor and said,

"Just do not look too beautiful tonight or you are going to have trouble with me."

Nathan had a little black female poodle in the house and named the dog Lady. On my way downstairs, Lady kept wiggling herself around me. I called Nathan and said,

"Nathan, Lady's hair got all over my clothes."

Nathan rushed to the staircase where I was standing and with one hand brushing the poodle's hair down and with the other hand shaking my pants. Nathan immediately apologized for his poodle shedding hair and said,

"I am so sorry my dear. Let me brush the dog's hair off."

I kidded with Nathan, and said,

"Is lady an American or Vietnamese?"

"It is an American lady, my love." Nathan replied.

I asked him,

"When did you get lady to move in the house with you?"

Nathan replied,

"I got lady to move in the house after I got back home from Vietnam. The Vietnamese lady is the one standing before me."

I was wearing Sharlimar perfume, when I walked by Nathan. He complimented,

"You smell so good, my dear"

"I smell so good because I eat rice." I kidded with him.

Nathan added,

"And fish heads also."

The two of us started laughing. I said to Nathan,

"You are funny, Nathan."

When his friends arrived, the four of us left for the Japanese Steak House in downtown Washington. The weekend I spent with Nathan was great because Nathan was always nice and cordial to me, except he did not give me the love I needed from him.

The next morning we had a breakfast together at his home. Nathan grasped my hand and asked me to marry him. He said there is a college near his home and I could go to school there to learn creative writing. He said,

"Your book will be worthwhile if you study creative writing. You do not have to work. Only go to school and be with me and I will take care of you. You help me rearrange the furniture in the house and pick out some new pieces of furniture that you think would look good for the house. After school, you just do some shopping and look around and do what you please."

I looked at Nathan in his hazel nut eyes and with regret, I said,

"Nathan, we have a problem. When we sleep together, your reaction to me is inadequate. The whole first week of your visit with me in Maine was the same incomplete situation. I am confused about our relationship. How did you react with Adriane? I felt sad because I can not understand why I do not arouse you!"

Nathan seemed concerned with my reaction and said,

"April is too much of a woman, which is why I am having a problem reacting to you. Give me more time to adjust to you. I want to marry you and I want you to have my life insurance."

"I can not marry you and have sex with someone else, Nathan. That is not my moral standards. I do not want my husband to be without physical love." I explained.

Nathan was six foot two, well built, and good looking. He was very alert about many things. He was thirty-two years old. He was a successful C.I.A. person.

I flew back to Maine on Sunday afternoon. I had a few more months to finish my schooling there. Nathan told me to get ready to come to Virginia at the end of my school year.

As the school year was about to close, I wrote to André in Bloomington, Illinois. His mother wrote me that he was no longer there. He was in Oklahoma City with his friend, Hunter Johnston, whom had returned to the United States from Vietnam about a couple months earlier than André. Hunter had brought a Vietnamese girlfriend back home with him. Back in Saigon, Hunter was interested in me even though he was chasing a number of girls; he still thought that he could get me also. Therefore, in my opinion, Hunter was just a playboy from Oklahoma. Instead of writing André a letter, I decided to call

149

him using the telephone number his mother gave me. When I got him on the phone, André asked me to come to Oklahoma City to meet him. Three days later I received a round trip ticket to Oklahoma.

I arrived at Oklahoma City in the summer of 1976. André met me at the airport and said,

"The American jet has delivered my precious cargo to Roger Airport in Oklahoma City." André was kidding about me as his precious cargo when he hugged me.

André had a nice and disarming smile. When he smiled he could take away my nostalgia. André asked,

"Do you want to get something to eat?"

I was not worried about his mockery. I was thinking how he was going to answer to his conscience about what he had done. I replied,

"I am starving. Let us go eat. I will buy."

André grinned with a sense of humor,

"My wife is using my money to buy me a meal?"

I did not like his joke, but we went into a restaurant in the airport. When we sat down at the table, I ordered a Miller Lite and veal parmesan. André ordered a Michelob beer and deluxe hamburger. Look at what he ordered. I knew how much of an American he was. He was one of the most snobbish and obnoxious Americans on this planet. He laughed over your pain when you needed someone to talk to. I looked at him and asked,

"You are always mysterious, André. If I did not care about you, I would not keep up with you. Did you have a plot to transport human cargo to the United States? Were you a part of it? Where is my cut, André?"

André was sitting there stuffing himself with his deluxe hamburger. He gulped down the beer then explained,

"April, I did it for reasons of humanitarianism. I helped to rescue people form war zones, just as in Iran, Lebanon, and Argentina."

I went on,

"Are you telling me that the Shell Corporation president's family stepped into the plane with five large suitcases — and this was nothing? And they gave you one of the suitcases as a token of their thanks. I was your partner and signed the papers for them, André. Do not bullshit me anymore. I am sick and tired of your phony baloney. So cut it out. How about giving me a lump sum so I can do something with my life in America?"

At this point, he bribed me by a kiss on my hand and comforted me with,

"April, do you want to see a movie? If we leave the restaurant now, we will not be late for the show. I had made a reservation before hand."

* * *

André took me to see his friend, Hunter Johnston. He was a staff member of the DAO, a branch of the American Embassy in South Vietnam. Hunter was divorced and had a young daughter named Sara Goodfriend whom was twenty-four years old. She was married and her husband was a year older than her. He was a big guy but with Sara he was like a teddy bear. When we all sat in the car to go shopping at the mall downtown, her husband was the driver but Sara was the backseat driver! While he was driving, Sara constantly shouted at her husband about his steering. The whole time in the car Sara never let up on her husband. She used profanity to instruct her husband how to drive the car. One of the times she shouted out,

"Goddamn it! Can you drive with the steering wheel straight and hold your hands on it."

During the whole time Sara was constantly noisy in the car. André was uneasy about Sara's hollering. André asked me,

"You have not learned anything?"

"I do not know. I am just a new arrival here in Oklahoma. I know one thing; I do not want to be a loud bitch." I answered.

Inwardly I despised Sara. She was not a pleasant American woman at all. How could her husband put up with her? In some cases, maybe, Sara's screaming would impress some women who would like to be a Hitler. I believed in fairness and mutual respect which would bring a happier situation in both the wife and husband's daily lives.

My visit to Oklahoma City had ended with no solution to what my 'partner' had done with my share. I flew back to Maine in order to get ready for school in Atlanta, Georgia. It was really strange that I felt empty about André. Nothing was there between us even though he was nice and warm the whole time I was in Oklahoma City with him. Something was fishy about André. He was not totally honest with me about my cut.

XI

Hard Time / Conquering

I thought everything was alright until my car developed a terminal illness. I drove it for two weeks before I discovered that it was badly rusted. The first bill came two weeks after I had purchased the car. I paid forty-nine dollars and thirty-five cents for new sparkplugs, points, and a couple other things.

Subsequently, my car kept failing in health. The gas tank developed a leak and the battery needed replacement and the wiring caught fire. The bumper fell off along with other parts, one after another. Finally, my car's doctor suggested giving it a decent burial in the junkyard. I was very sad when I heard the car's prognosis. How can I save another fifteen hundred dollars in a short while to purchase another car?

I called the person who sold me the car and asked him if he knew about the condition of the car prior to purchase. I asked him,

"Mr. Fisher, did you know about the condition of the car prior to purchase?"

Mr. Fisher answered,

"I sold the car to you without a guarantee. You bought it as is."

I said,

"I told you that I am a student and new in the country. I do not have that much money. But I need a good running car and you told me it was a good car."

"It was a good car when you bought it but after you drove, that is another story. How do I know what you did to the car after purchasing it?" Mr. Fisher said.

I asked,

"Can you give me some money back because the car was only driven for three months?"

"I am sorry about the car. I can not give you any money back."

That was the end of the saga of my car.

One time when there was a heavy downfall of snow, the car skidded into a telephone pole because the road was so icy. My car was coming down the hill at twenty-five miles an hour, and then suddenly the speedometer showed thirty-five miles an hour. I set my foot on the brake to slow the car. The whole car body started spinning and I lost control. The belt was not fastened and fortunately my head did not hit the windshield when I collided with the telephone pole. Two police patrol cars immediately arrived there to help me at the accident scene. They told me that it was a miracle that I did not get hurt. The front end on the driver's side came in about ten inches and crushed the radiator. One of the policemen told me to drive the car to a body shop in town where they might fix it for a reasonable price.

After the accident, many of my friends joked with me that they wanted to know when I drive my car on the road, so they would park their cars in the garage, and I would have the whole road to myself. When the policeman saw me in the damaged car, he asked me if I drove the car or shot it. I received many compliments about the beauty of my car. One of them said, if I hit all the way around it would match the dents of the car. This gave me uneasy feeling, but here again I was learning how people joke in America.

My younger stepbrother worked in a local restaurant until it closed its doors due to a lack of business. I was saddened by the loss of his job. Prior to that time, he was supporting himself and then I was ready to leave Maine. When I explained my problem to a friend, she told me that I reminded her of a person digging a hole while standing in it. The deeper one digs the harder it is to get out of the hole. I then returned to my apartment to decide how I might gain a foothold in order to get out of the deep hole I had dug. After some deep thought, we found a solution. My younger step-brother went to Atlanta, Georgia to further his education at Georgia Tech.

People are the most interesting creatures in the world, but also the most complicated.

As time went by, I continued to help the four Vietnamese and their communication with their sponsor. For awhile, the four regained their balance of thought and spirit which they had temporarily lost because of the long ordeal that they had gone through. Later these men accused me of being too Americanized. They believed that I was too independent. I was supposed to remain a traditional Vietnamese woman dependent upon Vietnamese men. How could I be dependent on them? When they were not independent, I begin to spend less time with them. This made the men furious and blamed each other for causing my absence. I was sad about this.

Oriental people are very sensitive. Even though these men had gone through hardships, it was hard for them to accept the position in which they found themselves. They were unable to repay the kindness being shown them by the people in Limestone who assisted them from the time of their arrival.

When they arrived in Maine, it was summer time. The first job the four had was harvesting potatoes. They arose and went to the fields at five in the morning and they came home at five in the afternoon. Their sponsor, due to his job, had to be absent one week out of every three weeks. I drove them back and forth to work and from work everyday. I also shared food and small talk with them, and I was their interpreter.

But this local welfare support was misunderstood by these four young men. One day one of the young men was saddened and got drunk and threatened to kill me. I had become the symbol of what he wanted to be —— 'Americanized.'

I visited the four Vietnamese to see if they needed to see their sponsor at Loring Air Force Base. They were drinking beer. Nguyên, the youngest man said,

"April must be the sweetest girl of her family. She is always decent."

Chiêm Khén chimed in,

"You know, good family upbringing had a lot to do with her present personality. She is from a good family. Why are you not married, April?"

"I do not know exactly what I will be doing. How can I think of getting married? Most of you have a wife back home except, Nguyên. He is young like my brother. So forget the question about when I am getting married."

Chiêm Khén, the oldest, had quite a few beers earlier. He picked up a dinner knife, pointed at me and said,

"You are too Americanized April. You come and go as you please. I want to stick this knife into your stomach to see how much Americanized you are."

I said quickly,

"You confuse me, Chiêm Khén. All I have done for you guys is to help you out. But if you do not consider that was my help then I am sorry."

The other two young men grasped Chiêm Khén and pulled him back as I ran out and jumped in my car and drove to see the captain at Loring Air Force Base.

When I arrived at the base, I went inside to the security officer and asked to see Gus. A few minutes later, Gus walked into the waiting room. I said,

"We have a problem. The four young men got drunk and Chiêm Khén threatened my life with a dinner knife. He slurred "you are too Americanized." I quickly jumped in my car to let you know."

Captain Blackwell's face looked stern, and he said,

"April. Would you translate a letter in Vietnamese to the guys? They need to know that I will do anything to help them, but they must stop this stupid action which might jeopardize their future."

After I translated Captain Blackwell's letter intended for the young men. Gus advised me to take my girlfriend Judy with me to deliver his letter to them. Gus said,

162

"I will be coming home tomorrow. Please let the guys know that I will see them soon."

It was four thirty in the afternoon and I used the phone in the waiting room to call Judy at work to ask her if she could stop by the alert facility building to see me and Gus.

When Judy arrived, Gus told her what happened between me and the guys. He asked Judy to go with me to his house to give the guys his letter of condemnation.

Shortly after, Judy and I arrived at Gus's home, I handed the letter to the four young men from Gus which I had translated into Vietnamese. This is an excerpt of what he wrote:

"One of the reasons I sponsored you was to show other Americans that the South Vietnamese people were worth fifty thousand American lives to save. But just as during the war, we cannot fight all your battles for you.

You are a small Vietnamese life boat on a large American ocean. You need each other and you have to have one another. You cannot survive if you do not have this. It is apparent you do not like April. That is your right. Her words are my words. You are accusing her of something you must become..."

Their sponsor was an intelligent man. His words were pointed. He wounded the men without a weapon.

After I translated the letter for them, the men felt ashamed.

They felt they had acted poorly. I explained to them that time would repair their mistake.

The above occurrence reminded me of a Vietnamese folk story.

Many years ago there was a king who had a very loyal and faithful general. One day, the general committed a small mistake. The king stated that the mistake of the faithful general demonstrated a lack of loyalty to the king. To show the king his loyalty to his country, the general committed suicide. The king lost his faithful general.

These men were former military men. They had been unable to save their home or homeland, and had barely escaped with their lives. Now they were in the home of a military man of another country. This man was not only their sponsor, but had become a father figure to them. As a loving father he was willing to forgive them, but his words had cut to the quick.

Their shame of injuring their sponsor caused them to voluntarily leave the captain's home. Two of them left for Colorado where they went to work. The other two moved into an apartment after finding jobs in another Maine community, one of these two continued his education in night school.

The kindness of their sponsor is still remembered and appreciated, I am certain. They would like to regain his respect. In the letters I have received from these young men reflect their hope of this.

The departure of these men was a disappointment to me. It ruined my efforts to help them blend into American society, as I had my own difficulties. Therefore, I understood what these young men were going through. For this reason I benefited from their experiences in relationship to my own life adjustment.

Since I came from the same culture as those young men, their behavior was a part of my responsibility. If they did wrong, it reflected on the rest of my people. However, I hope we are not all judged as a group (stereotyping). People make mistakes worldwide. I can only hope that they have learned from their misdeed, and have become more moral citizens.

Due to the bad water in Caribou, I frequently became sick in my stomach and had something like convulsions plus diarrhea. During that time the Richardsons came around to make sure that I was alright, especially, Wilma Richardson. Wilma was like an angel from heaven and came to aid me at my sick bed. The last time I called Wilma up to let her know that I had difficulty breathing; she drove to my apartment and took me to Caribou Memorial Hospital at once! My doctor was from India, and he prescribed medicine, and then comforted me with,

"You will get used to it, April. When I first came to America, my body system went through the same kind of changes."

The doctor told me to get spring water at a hill near Caribou until the city fixed the broken pipes in town. After that, Wilma was so considerate that she asked me to move to her family's home. Her oldest daughter Cindy was away from home attending school in Delaware. I was lucky to receive her help and allowed to stay at Richardson's happy family home. In a few weeks I would be on my way to Atlanta, Georgia.

As usual, I drove with Wilma to go and get the spring water up the hill only this time we met two Japanese young men in a van which was heading toward downtown Caribou. Their van had a flat tire where Wilma and I were getting our spring water. By the end of the conversation, the older Japanese man introduced himself to us as a regional manager with the International Unification Religion in New York. He had an intellectual look, wearing gold rim reading glasses, well groomed, tall and had a healthy complexion. He invited me to attend the speech of Reverend Sung Young Moon on the two hundredth birthday of the founding of United States of America at Yankee Stadium on June 6, 1976 in New York. He asked me to give him my mailing address so he could mail me a plane ticket to New York.

Prior to leaving Maine, my younger stepbrother called me to let me know that he had found himself a full time job with a Chinese restaurant and was accepted as a full time student at Georgia Tech. He asked me to come to Atlanta so we could help each other. He was the only brother I had in America so I decided to come to Atlanta that summer in 1976.

After some thought, I called Nathan up and told him that I was going to Atlanta, Georgia. This caused him great concern so he told me to stop at the Virginia National Airport on my way to Georgia to see him. My airplane landed at the airport. I walked inside the glass door and saw Nathan and Adriane together on the escalator as it rolled down to where I was standing. Because of Adriane's presence with Nathan, I felt I should continue my flight alone to New York. I was on my way to New York to attend a religious rally at Yankee Stadium. I was a guest there on a one week all expenses paid tour. This was paid by the Unification Church.

XII

Back to Back for Success

Back to the old time in Saigon, Adriane was twenty-three years old when she was the President of CEDEFEXCO, Asia Bicycle Manufacturer Company of South Vietnam. We were best friends. It is wonderful not only to be young but successful. To be successful at a younger age, one must not only work hard but be very smart and have good luck. Without these vital fundamentals, you are not going to make it. She also was publishing Director of Tidal Wave newspaper in Saigon city. Everyone who lived in Saigon had heard of the well known newspaper, a newspaper of the South Vietnamese people with integrity and honesty. Many times the government tried to shut down the entire newspaper because it was the eyes of the people and exposed the corruption and bribery within the Saigon government. A friend of Adriane, who was an eminent writer, Mai Thao of the South, had been beaten up a number of times by the secret police. The government wanted to put him to death. He meant more to the government than a hundred Vietnamese Communists with AK riffles, rockets, and M-16"s. He was a writer in South Vietnam. Adriane's newspaper "Tidal Wave" was an appropriate name indeed.

Adriane met Nathan at a special occasion one weekend; they had a party at the United States Marine Building. Since I was Adriane's friend and her sales manager for CEDEFEXCO, I was invited. There I met André. He was the Chief of Personnel for the DAO, a branch of the United States Embassy in Saigon. After André and I became friends, Adriane objected to my relationship with him. Adriane did not think very highly of André. So my relationship with André was only between the two of us. We could not go where Adriane was, such as parties and personal meetings. Adriane and I were very close friends. We did not share our men, but we did share almost everything like money, luck, and our success.

Nathan was an Intelligent Specialist for the Central Intelligent Agency (CIA) in Saigon. Nathan's job was to spot the targets for B-52s to drop bombs in North Vietnam. Nathan always gave me first class treatment and made me feel good. Adriane did not have any suspicions or jealousy about the way Nathan treated me. Then we met at the National Virginia Airport some years ago, that was when Nathan proposed to me.

I was not in a position to get married to anyone. I was feeling depressed about my life and future in the United States. Where would I be living? Who could I trust? What would I be? A number of questions were on my mind. I was worried about how could I take care of myself. Also, I was concerned about the welfare of my family in Vietnam.

When I met Adriane, I was personnel manager of Vinnell Corporation in Saigon. Adriane was one of the two hundred applicants for a position of controller with the company. My heart felt glad when I first saw Adriane in my office. Something about this young lady touched my heart through her gestures and her distinguished personality. I gave her an application form and told her to fill it out and come back to see me tomorrow because I told her I wanted to hire her.

Adriane left my office. That same afternoon, Adriane got an offer from the CRA, a branch of the American Embassy, for a position as a financial administrator. Two days later I got a phone call from Adriane for a luncheon appointment with her. At lunch, Adriane recommended me for General Manager of a one-thousand seat dining room with games and a swimming pool as part of the CRA. She explained,

"Mr. Cardin is our big boss. He gave me the authorization of hiring a crew in this position. If you accept my offer, I will let you hire your own crew. Your salary will be double what you are making at Vinnell Corporation. You impressed me very much at your office when you promised me a job with your company. April, please come and join our team. I loved you the moment I talked with you."

I replied,

"I have never worked in the restaurant business and I am not qualified for the job. Why don't you look for someone else, Adriane?"

Adriane insisted

"April, please give me a chance to do something for you. Please work with me for a while then we will start our career while we are very young. Believe me! I can not tell you why now, just have faith in me. For whatever reason, you will get all the assistance from Mr. Cardin and me. You have got that from us. We will back you up."

Two years later, big and small wheels in the telecommunication system in the American Embassy of fifteen hundred personnel turned over. A new group moved in and took over their jobs. Mr. Cardin resigned from his position and Adriane started CEDEFEXCO Asia Bicycle Manufacturer, Inc.

I was asked to stay on the job as manager of C.R.A. A Bob Barton was assigned as a replacement for Mr. Cardin. On the job for about three months, Bob suggested that he would buy a diamond ring for me. I declined his offer and problems began. Bob had the background of a lowly and vulgar American boy. He started his career in the American Army mess hall as a hamburger cook. Since I would not wear his diamond, he bought the ring and put it on the finger of one of my waitresses. His defying attitude made him look smaller. One afternoon in the office, Bob put his hand on my shoulder. I politely knocked it off my shoulder. Bob became furious and dropped himself down in the wing chair and started a downpour on me. He said,

"Have you seen in the news this morning that a man walked in the Post Office with his briefcase of money and got shot in the chest three times? And there are lootings right here in town? You Vietnamese are crooks!"

I said,

"Bob, listen to this. The lootings in town are small compared to the biggest crook right here in this office. Your liquor business with CRA so far is successful. Every ten dollars worth of liquor you order from the United States is tax exempt. You make a ninety dollar profit on the purchase. You refund the expense account of CRA and make large purchases of liquor. Your trucks of liquor drop off a small quantity in CRA and then go to town to the distributors. Now, it is up to you. I can walk out of here and tomorrow the front page of the newspaper will

174

have your name in the headlines: "Biggest crook in the American Embassy." It is your American dollars and you do what you feel you want to do about it. But at least the American people back home are entitled to know where their tax money went? I did not see your trucks of liquor until you made the above statement, Bob. Just cool off, things are not that bad. You and your son live in a nice area and have a money-making job. Just take it easy on the people working for you. They leave you alone so leave them alone.

A year later I left the CRA as dining room manager to join Adriane's Asia Bicycle Manufacturer, Inc. My international restaurant business with a live show nightly started that year.

XIII

A Triangle Love

Time slipped by almost an incredible year and a half. I left Maine to relocate in Atlanta starting in the summer of 1976.

I called Nathan in Virginia to see how he and Adriane were doing. Nathan told me that Adriane was insanely jealous and caused him a lot of heartache. Nathan asked me if he could come down to see me for two weeks. He was still thinking of me. Since Nathan, Adriane and I had so many things to share together, going back to the old times in Vietnam was alright with me.

Nathan came alone and stayed two weeks with me. We ate and laughed together. But the problem of no love in the bedroom still existed. He seemed to have an impotence problem with me. Why? I do not know. Why was Adriane, after all these years, still with him? Nathan still wanted to marry me and get transferred to Atlanta so he could be with me. I did not understand why we should be together as man and wife with no physical intimacy between us. I said,

"No Nathan. It will not work. How could we get married and not make love. You would not want to see me having another man. Besides, you just cannot seem to respond to me."

Nathan went back to Virginia. Three months later, I received a phone call from André to let me know that Adriane shot Nathan to death and he was gone for good now. A couple of years later I saw Adriane in Atlanta in an ice cream parlor inside of the building where I worked. Adriane was working for Western Union as an accountant.

To have met Adriane in Atlanta was an incredible surprise. We were the best friends many years back home in Saigon. I was sitting with a news reporter, a new friend, I met in town. Seeing Adriane at the other table, still beautiful in disguise, my heart was pumping in my chest. It had been so long since I saw Adriane last time at the National Virginia Airport in Virginia. I heard that many people change after they do not see someone for a while, especially people in the United States. I was not sure how I would approach her. Finally, I got up and walked toward her table and introduce myself to her. The brief moments we saw each other, I saw tears in her eyes.

"April, how have you been?"

We sat down while my news reporter friend at the other table jotted down something in his notebook.

Adriane remarked: "I loved the man, who wanted to marry you, April."

I felt something stuck in my throat. After all these years of our friendship, Adriane was still very suspicious of my love for her.

I explained,

"I and Nathan were friends. There was no sex involved between us. Nathan was a free man. He had the right to aim his direction, or goals where he wanted to, totally up to him. I did not get Nathan involved with me. I do not want a man that does not want me."

Adriane snapped at me,

"There, you see! You said it all. Nathan wanted you while seeing me for a year."

I felt a knot tie in my stomach when Adriane persistently did not hear me. I tried to explain to her,

"I am not a thief, Adriane. You are accusing me of something I have not done. I still love you like my own sister and wish all the best for you."

I asked.

"Why did you shoot Nathan? He was a fine man and a top CIA job."

When I asked her about this tragedy, she was sad and told me it was a long story. Adriane had changed and was not the same person I knew in Vietnam. She had become a smoker and seemed entirely different.

Adriane remained in a quiet position and threw her eyes out to the glass windows of the ice cream parlor. She then asked,

"Have you met Dee? I have learned that she is going to San Antonio University in Texas to finish her Master's degree. If you

179

love me, do not deal with her. She pissed me off when she tried to get my businesses in Saigon."

Back in those days of thunder in Saigon, Adriane, Dee and I were the best of friends. I always accommodated Adriane in every way possible, but not Dee. Dee was an immense challenge to Adriane. She was sharp looking and had a keen mind. She graduated from Saigon University with a degree in commercial business. She was practicing her degree with Adriane in her business.

One Saturday afternoon, the Chief of personnel in the American Embassy, invited Adriane, Dee and I to a cocktail party to discuss the sale of bicycles for his personnel in the office. He employed ninety people. If Adriane could make this connection with the Chief, she could make this large sale. While everybody was wining and dining in the large swimming pool area, Dee, in her seductive manner, went to the other side of the pool, took off her dress, leaving only her bikini on while the Chief was looking directly at her. He was hypnotized by her alluring body. The Chief left his guests and walked toward where Dee was standing. None of us had prepared for the occasion and had not worn our swimming suits. So Dee stole the whole show on that Saturday.

The sale of bicycles was discontinued in our discussion with the Chief. Since then Adriane despised Dee. A pretty woman is a deadly weapon. She turned the Chief upside down and inside out without physically touching him. Dee defeated Adriane and the rest of the guests successfully. The Chief spent the whole afternoon talking with Dee. She knew how to use what she had - the power of her body.

In reality, if things had worked out well between Nathan and I, I would care nothing about what Adriane had accused me of which was the stealing of her man. Nathan's choice was to marry me, not her. However, I was her right-hand business person. I advised her in business and handled advertising sale and financial arrangements. We spent much time together in our private lives in Saigon as well. I always felt very special about Adriane and her delicate personality. I said,

"Adriane, why don't we have dinner at my place tomorrow evening? We have lots of things to talk about, right?"

Adriane replied in a relaxed manner,

"I will have to call you for directions tomorrow, because I will not get off work until five in the evening."

Adriane was always so close to my heart it was impossible for me to get upset with her. I knew she wanted to think about whether she should have dinner with me at my place or maybe she would just sadly vanish because of the death of Nathan. I used every ounce of my love for her to extend my warm welcome to her. I insisted,

"Whatever happens, you will always be my best friend and I hope you feel the same. I missed you the whole time while here in America. When I first learned that you were in Virginia, I called Nathan in order to get in touch with you, but you were not available. After that, I had to go on with my life in Atlanta, and I still hoped that someday we would be together again."

I saw the old glow of happiness in her eyes. She then softly spoke to me,

"You look good, April! You must be feeling good about your life in America. But me, I am not very happy with the changes in my life and I just wish that I did not have to suffer anymore. I want to go with God! [1] You were the shadow who stole the light. Nathan was all I ever had, April!"

Tears dropped from her eyes which moved me because I also was experiencing the same feelings from the loss of our fortunes and life styles back in old Vietnam. I comforted her with,

"Money comes and money goes. We made it before, we will make it again. It will take us sometime to get it back. Please do not be in despair. We are instead alive in America, thank God! Think about the great suffering so many of our country men have experienced in the hands of the North Vietnamese Communist."

[1] In Vietnam, people wanted to die. "They want to go with God."

Adriane responded,

"I will call you tomorrow evening. Now I have to go back to work. I do not know if I will stay in Atlanta. I have expensive furniture in storage and I must decide where I prefer to stay. My company will pay all the expenses of moving to any city that I want to live and work in. I will talk to you tomorrow."

Welcome to Aroostook

April with Gus and four Vietnamese refugees.

I escorted a wife and her three children of an American man who had
to stay back in Saigon. He was fearful for his family's safety.

The camp I stayed at while in Guam.

At the camp in Guam.

In Guam, from left: Surey, Dee, US Navy guard and April.

April as a model for Yamaha motorcycle manufacturer in Japan at
nineteen years old.

The Marine's nineteenth birthday at the American Embassy. This was my first boyfriend. I was twenty-three.

At my restaurant in 1974 with friends. From left: André, me, and the embassy staff.

Heidi and April at my birthday party in my restaurant.

My restaurant workers and friends from the embassy at my birthday party.

My girl friends and also my employees at the embassy party.

Adriane at twenty-one.

Melenie and me at seventeen.

Melenie and me at seventeen.

Heide, the one who had two million liters of gasoline.

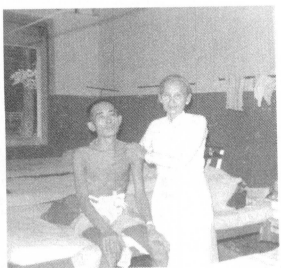

My mother holding up one of my brothers in the hospital. War almost
killed all my brothers in our family.

At sixteen as a singer on stage.

At seventeen as a singer on stage.

At eighteen in front of our home.

April at twenty-one.

Our family home in Saigon before the end of the war.

I was fifteen when 20th Century Fox wanted me to go to Hollywood.

April at seventeen.

At sixteen on a commercial vessel on Saigon River.

My younger brother in his banana garden.

My eighty-six year old mother and her grandchild.

At forty-six years old, still singing in the Saigon Club in 1994.

April in a Japanese kimono.

At nineteen in Tokyo, Japan.

199

Sister of Haruhiko and I on a tour of Tokyo.

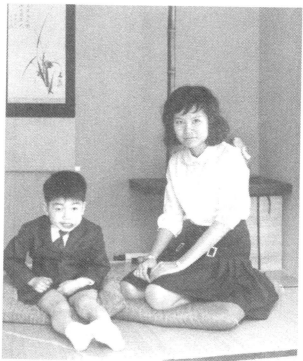

Japanese home of the Tokyo journalist.

Maine! In the parking lot outside our apartment, Rick and I.

The Richardson's and I in Maine.

Gus and his mother at home in Greensboro, NC.

At twelve years old when I cut the barbwire on my post.

After 20 years of being away, I finally met mother and family for the first time since 1974.

All my family greeting me at the airport in Saigon in 1994.

April and the red sneaker shoe guy. He is my world renowned
teacher. I am his masterpiece of art for twenty-three years. He is now
seventy years young.

April and restaurant staff at the CRA club

花ときそうベトナムのメイト

In a Japanese magazine, model for Yamaha Motorcycle advertisement. Japanese Headline reads: "The flowers compete with beautiful Vietnamese lady."

April at the beach - 1966 – then.

And now – 2001.

The man in the red sneaker shoes at 55 years of age.

April with her younger brother soldier in Saigon.

At the age of nineteen relaxing at home. My cousin took this picture
of me by surprise.

April's mother – 1966. A Deacon of her temple

April's mother with grandchild. Now 2002, 86 years old

April's deceased father.

XIV

Doubtful Mind

Wednesday evening came and Adriane called me at my apartment. She wanted the direction to my place for dinner. I was glad she did not change her mind about meeting me again. Nevertheless, the death of Nathan did bother me. Why did she shoot the bullet on such a loving Nathan? Why had she become an awesome killer? Will she shoot me too because I was an icon to Nathan when he was living? All those questions were going around in my head prior to Adriane's arrival. This is going to be a very touchy matter and I must be extremely careful as to what I have to say to Adriane when she shows up. If I slip up and say a wrong word I will never find out why she shot Nathan and I will loose her as my best friend. She was one of the best young business women in Vietnam, and because she was my best friend, Adriane was too valuable to loose. Also, her achievements back in Saigon were incredible. In addition her charity contributions were enormous and she was a firm believer in God — Adriane believed her success came from God's help. Therefore, Adriane often found herself in prayer at temples or churches for moral support and inspiration. Money never had been a problem to her back then. What bothered her most was the politics in Vietnam which had caused so much turmoil in business sales and manufacturing. If the gold prices decreased then rice and other crops increased. Thus productions such as automobiles, gasoline, kerosene, including Asia Bicycles, etc., experienced the same fate as gold values. In time of recession in the country, average people worried about their empty stomach, and the value of gold so much sale production had stopped. In this way the government of South Vietnam may have exercised the pressure to encourage the production of business thus being able to raise taxes. These changes continuously took place on a regular basis. Unfortunately in the later years, their approach caused businesses to suffer a great deal. Every time there was a change, the Asia Bicycles Manufacturing Company had to lower prices to get sales and thus lower monthly payments from our clients resulting in all around lower profits on parts and deliveries, etc. The war in Vietnam was one of the main sources of much of the business expansion in the cities but also created a headache for all of us, the Vietnamese entrepreneurs.

The door bell rang so I opened the door to greet Adriane. With usual femininity, Adriane walked gracefully through the door. I showed her in the living room. After all the changes in our lives, Adriane still had a hot and charming look about her. Men from all over the country and world she met in our business contacts in Saigon wanted to be her a knight with a spear riding on a big horse after her and wanted to kidnap her and carry her in their arms to their castle. They kidded with her that she was like a burning cast iron bar. When Adriane actually sat down, I studied her carefully. Her hair was long and down to her lovely shoulders and it was combed straight back with curly ends under and behind both ears. She had a beautifully shaped nose and her eyes had a continuous glow projecting with energy and enthusiasm. But most importantly was her shapely set of lips which always invited kisses, also she was able to transform those adorable lips to give business orders and commands. She never ignored any of my words, no matter how small, and she always gave me the feeling of putting me at a very high level. Before I sat down, I handed Adriane a glass of Sherry wine. We both loved Sherry because it has a smooth taste and light in alcohol. In the living room with just the two of us, I felt a return of so much blessing of our friendship thinking of those days in Saigon when we were together in important business meetings and our personal dancing parties and fun which seemed to last endlessly. Adriane lovingly asked,

"Do you have a boy friend that you really care for? I guess you must have a dozen men after you. April, not only are you sharp but also very sexy."

I used a little humor with Adriane and replied,

"I have admirers. Some have the looks but no brains. Others have brains but no looks."

Adriane queried,

"How do you know the right guy?"

I replied,

"The guy that my body wants is not the one. But the one that my heart desires he is the right guy."

Adriane continued,

"After all these years have you found the right one?"

I responded,

"I had found a man that had my love, affection, respect and more. He also had my most admiration. He did not smoke, drink, gamble nor whore around. He did every possible thing to help me, except to marry me. The reason he did not marry me was because I was poor at the time. I had never thought that material goods could interfere with a potential good marriage in America. I did not have a twenty thousand dollar living room suit like you had, Adriane. I had a good job to go to, some clothes and my book.

Time flies and things change. Now I am a land baron. I own the two most beautiful homes on the block. I have some money, not a whole lot, but I am comfortable. I have built three of the nicest homes for my three brothers in Vietnam. At this point, I am really very satisfied with the accomplishments I have made for my family, especially for my mother. She raised me with all the finest ingredients she found and learned in our lifetime."

Adriane responded,

"Your mother is a respectful lady. Every time I visited your family, I felt at home. She was warm and very loving with me."

I reassured,

"My mother loves you like she loves me. In her eyes you are another daughter."

With a smile, Adriane philosophized,

"Do you think American men are good looking and seductive? They are very masculine, but soft and tender with women."

I reinforced her opinion sharply,

"You are right. Generally speaking, American men are well-built. Their legs and arms are lethal weapons but not for violent purposes. They are normally happy and not very picky. They are persuasive."

I joked.

Adriane cordially suggested,

"I am new in town and do not know many people here. I wish we had a couple good male companions to be with us. Do you have any ideas?"

Adriane was always sharp and polite with me because she knew that she could only bend a steel bar but breaking it was not possible. She bent my mind with her sweet ways and meekness, so she persuaded me to go out of my way to do things for her or for us. And of course Adriane succeeded with her objectives most of the time. I replied,

"I need to make a couple phone calls. Can you wait for a few minutes?"

Adriane answered,

"Yes April, you are absolutely unbeatable. How could anyone say no to you?"

I looked in my address book, with my mind searching, from A to Z for all the male friends that I knew. Finally, I stopped at two — Aga and Baba. Aga was from Argentina, he was a businessman with a German international trading company which was headquartered in Atlanta. His company sold all kinds of food items and other merchandise such as furniture, lamp shades, etc. He sold them to all the Caribbean islands. He was in his early 30s, single, about medium sized with a masculine appearance and was well tanned. He was a typical South American with his physical traits.

Baba was a Panama consul whom I had met once a week in his office to take care of the paperwork in shipping commodities from Atlanta to Panama for my company. He was forty, divorced and had two young children. He was tall, physically fit and well dressed. He greeted me with a smile all the time and he signed my papers before anybody else. Thus the commercial vessels could leave the docks on time with the proper paperwork for clearance and insurance in case of spoilage. This was imperative because of the many instances when perishable shipments were at stake. Thus Baba and I became acquainted. He grew to like me better. One day I was visiting his office and he asked me to go to dinner and dancing at a fine club in Atlanta.

I dialed the phone number and said,

"Hello, is Baba there?"

I continued,

"How are you, what are you doing tonight?"

Baba answered,

"I am writing a letter home to Panama. What do you have in mind?"

I continued,

"Can you come over to my place? I have somebody very special that I would like you to meet. Her name is Adriane."

Baba replied,

"Sure, I will be glad to but with one condition." He joked, "Will you help me meet a beautiful Vietnamese high caliber lady to be my woman? Give me forty-five minutes to get ready."

"You got it." I said.

I then dialed Aga's phone number and a voice said, "Aga speaking."

I asked,

"Aga, can we get together at my place? I have a very special lady that I Would like you to meet?"

Aga responded inquisitively,

"Really? Is she beautiful like you? Then I will come over right now, I would love to see you and meet her."

I answered,

"Aga, you will not be disappointed. I promise! If you are anxious to see me then do what I say and you will meet my girlfriend."

I turned to Adriane and told her,

"Two men will be here shortly to keep us company. They are interesting people whom I met through work. You will like them. They are fine."

Adriane asked me with a cautious voice,

"Is this a treat or are you dumping them on me?"

I immediately replied,

"This is a treat for sure."

Both of us laughed together. Adriane said admiringly, "April, you have never been short of men!"

I modestly answered,

"You are right about that. I might have been short of money, but not men. I do not know why I am so lucky. Perhaps God knows men make my life more bearable."

Adriane with a smile, stated,

"You are so poetic. That is why you have so much femininity in you and why men come around you. I remember in the CRA, men from all levels, Colonel to Corporal, at the Embassy admired your intriguing personality. Most of the accomplishments at the CRA were from your achievement."

I explained,

"I trained my new employees with extensive orientation about the benefits they could get from being employed with us and the benefit from their loyalty to me as well. Their security of employment is guaranteed if they followed our rules and regulations. Of course, they all loved me but problems did arise from time to time amongst the seventy-five employees. But that is how I loved my challenges."

Aga and Baba showed up at the door. Both were in their business attire. I greeted the two men and introduced them to my friend Adriane. They shook hands and exchanged their business cards.

Aga and Baba paid Adriane their compliments,

"You are a beautiful lady, indeed"

Adriane gave the men a smile and thanked the two for their compliments,

"Thank you so much. You are so kind to me. April has good eyes to have such wonderful friends like you. We like professionalism in a man and you two gentlemen are the men."

I served drinks to our international business friends as they had conversation with Adriane. My mind was constantly thinking about the death of Nathan. Adriane was above the average woman. She has wits and good composure all the time since I have known her back in Saigon. I will have to use my best tact when talking with her about our loss of Nathan.

"How about some music and some soft light?" I suggested.

The "Song of Unchanged Melody" sang by the Righteous Brothers began and we danced. These two men from South America were very reserved. Their polite manner impressed Adriane. We felt the meeting was enjoyable for all of us. Meeting interesting people is far more enjoyable than cheap sex. Because smart women do not go for flip-flop men, hoping they will invest two cents in a relationship.

I turned to Adriane and asked,

"Why did you shoot Nathan, Adriane?"

Adriane looked with sorrow, and said,

"April, please do not talk about it. Can you forget the tragedy about Nathan and me? He was so sweet and such a gentleman that I could not think that his mind was concentrating on you. Then I realized that it is difficult or impossible to read somebody's mind. When I arrived in Virginia I found out that Nathan was going to transfer his job to Atlanta. The only reason I could think of why Nathan wanted to go was because you were in Atlanta. I disapproved of Nathan's move to Atlanta, so the argument began.

(She was so emotionally distraught that she was unable to adequately express her thoughts. Her passion overflowed to the point that her tears ran down her cheeks.)

"While we were in Nathan's bedroom, I jumped over Nathan and a struggle started between him and myself. Our bodies rolled off the bed together, at which time the gun fell off the end table onto the floor. At this point, when we hit the floor together, we both went for the gun and it went off, fatally wounding Nathan. He loved me, but he loved you more, April."

I asked Adriane,

"How were you able to convince the authorities that it was an accident?"

She replied,

"There was a jury trial and with proper legal representation, I was fortunately able to be exonerated."

Adriane's voice was full of anguish and had touched my heart. Her pretty eyes begged for mercy. Adriane had my support as always. But this time it was different. The incident of Nathan's mysterious demise bothered me. At that point I felt a cold wall between us. I did not get the answers from Adriane as to how something of such a terrible magnitude could have happened. I forcibly subdued my thoughts of questioning anymore. The puzzle of Nathan's death had been concealed with Adriane forever. Suddenly and unexpectedly, Adriane left Atlanta without saying goodbye. That was her way of telling me that I was the thief who had stolen Nathan's heart. In another words, I was her opponent all the time even when she saw me in Atlanta. Adriane wanted to squeeze the juices from my only innocent sin, which was that I was adored by Nathan. Adriane's powerful Confucian teachings had controlled her mind and made her very patient with me. She decided I was her enemy.

XV

Historical Events

Vietnamese nature is one of a peace loving people. Nevertheless, we defend for our love and possessions. Family ties in Vietnam are supreme because of the life-long existence of family and love that remains forever. The five thousand years of our Vietnamese history is that conjugal relationships are divine. An example of this follows in "The Value of a Promise."

A few centuries ago, what we know today as Vietnam was part of the kingdom of the learned Sở Bá Vuồng. His benevolent reign was ended when warring Mongols attacked, and after fierce fighting, overcame the country. The King was forced to flee from his palace. The vengeful Mongols pursued him, wishing to put him to death.

Finding his way blocked by a wide river, the King made his escape. He promised a ferry-man half his kingdom when he returned, and pushed back the Mongol invader.

Sở Bá Vuổng was a man of high reputation, known especially for his honesty and integrity. Thus he was able to regain his kingdom through the support of his people. He was able to form another army and win back his country.

The King married and was happy for a few years and all was peaceful. The incident at the river was forgotten. Then once again an invader with superior forces defeated the King's army. Once again he had to flee for his life, only this time he was accompanied by his beautiful and virtuous wife, the Queen.

As they approached the river, the same ferry-man appeared before the regal couple. He told the couple that his sampan was very small and could carry only one passenger. The Queen hearing this wept for her husband. He did not want to go on without her. While he talked with the ferry-man, she embraced him and quickly slipped away to commit suicide so that her husband might escape,

When he learned what she had done, Sở Bá Vủỏng heart-broken. And now, the ferry-man reminded the King of his unkept promise. The King realized how he had forgotten his word. So that he might make good his promise to the ferry-man, Sở Bá Vủỏng committed suicide.

The other king who was pursuing him had offered a reward of half his new kingdom for the man who captured Sở Bá Vủỏng. By delivering his body to the Mongol King, the ferry-man was able to claim half the kingdom which had been offered as a reward. In this way he became the ruler, and Sở Bá Vủỏng's promise was finally kept.

The moral of the story is: a man's word should be binding even unto death. One's promise should be made with careful deliberation before being spoken. Once spoken, it should be considered a binding contract.

This story of Sở Bá Vủỏng is traditional in Vietnam and has been popular throughout many, many generations. Today it remains part of the education of every young Vietnamese.

Another incident in our cultural history is when two women stepped forward during our struggle with China. The history of Vietnam goes back two thousand years.

There once were two ladies, Queens. They occupied the throne after pushing back the Chinese invaders to China. The two ruled the country for three years. Then again, the Chinese with their powerful forces invaded Vietnam. The Chinese army overcame the power of the two Ladies' army by fighting with all their clothes off. The Chinese armies were completely bare naked in the arena. They used psychological warfare to attack the Queens to win the war. The Chinese remained in Vietnam for a thousand years before they withdrew to the China mainland. The two committed suicide by jumping into the river. Today the names of these two are still in the memory of the younger generations. Names of the Vietnamese rulers are

Trưng Trắct and Trưng Nhị. There is a Trưng Sister Boulevard in Saigon (today Hồ Chí Minh City).

The Chinese leadership was amazed by the courage of the Vietnamese women and their patriotism to the Vietnamese people. The Chinese leaders proposed to the Tru'ngs, but they would rather die than marry their people's enemy.

Two thousand years ago death was victory. Today people have changed their thinking about life and death. Death can not accomplish anything good.

XVI

Torn Between Two Loves

"Captain Chad Cahill of the United States Marine Corp (USMC) in Virginia."

I was glad that I able to locate Chad. In Vietnam, Chad was Chief of Marine Security at the embassy in Saigon. I said,

"Hello Chad. This is April in the C.R.A. in Saigon. I got your phone number from USMC in Washington D.C."

Chad gasped,

"Hey! April, how are you? Where are you living now?"

I replied,

"I am now in Atlanta, Georgia working for a bank."

Chad mesmerized,

"April you are a woman that has no price tag. One evening on the weekend we went out to an Italian restaurant. We had a bottle of wine and you also have a dish of cheese. That was all it took to empty my wallet paying for the restaurant bill that evening." (In Vietnam we did not have credit cards at that time).

I teased Chad,

"And you told me that if you have any money left you would have taken me to a hotel. I was flattered that you desire me. But you were gentleman enough to take me home."

Chad pleaded,

"April, I promise that I will make it right this time. I thought how lovely you look every day at CRA all the time. Your mind was always busy with your job, and so did I. The embassy was under surveillance and security system around the clock, even though we slept with one eye opened. I live and work here in Virginia. If you come to Virginia, I will send you a round trip ticket and we will go to a steak house for dinner. Smart people eat steaks, right?"

The weekend came and I flew to Virginia. Chad drove a new covert to the airport to greet me. I liked Chad in USMC uniform better, but he was just wearing a navy blue blazer with creamy pants that day. He put his arms around me and kissed me on the lips. He asked,

"Was the flight bringing you to me pleasant?"

I smiled at Chad,

"Thank you, it was fine. I just do not have much appetite for the food on the plane because it was not a long trip from Atlanta."

Chad suggested,

"We will go to a bar and have some cocktail drinks and talk for old times sake. Then when the evening comes, we will eat dinner together. It is one year today that we finally are alone again. I have a two bedroom condo here in Virginia. I live alone. We will go over there after dinner to see if you like it."

I liked Chad and his ability to keep the embassy in the top security. With fifteen hundred personnel, it was not an easy job for him. Now that I am alone with Chad, I did not have any fear that anything might happened to me. Every personnel in the embassy had their security clearance checked back to ten years ago or longer. So, if you are with me, you are safe. If I am with the captain, I am pretty sure that I am safe with him, too. His statement about smart people eat steaks, in my opinion was correct. Because poor people do not know how to make money to afford New York steaks, etc.

We arrived at Chad's home. He has good taste in furnishing the place. It is clean and the air is fresh. Chad had never pushed me into doing anything that is not my desire. How smart this man was. He was smart because he ate steak. I teased him with my loving arms around him.

Sunday came around and I flew back to Atlanta. I remembered Chad told me that he will drive to Atlanta to see me soon.

Gus had been flying to Atlanta twice to see me from Maine. I like what Gus had done for the four Vietnamese sailors. But I did not like his messing around while I was true blue to him. I wanted Gus out of my system, but there was something about him that still clung on to me. I loved him a little bit and that little bit of feeling was constantly inside my heart. Chad was my way to get Gus out of my mind. But it did not work. I was too sentimental for Gus. He helped my fellow countrymen like his family. I adored Gus mostly for that reason.

After being stationed at Loring Air Force Base in Maine, Gus got his transfer orders to an Air Force base in California.

One evening Chad drove to Atlanta to see me. As the door closed behind us, Chad seized his arms around and whispered to my ear,

"God made the mold for you then He broke it."

Chad kissed me tenderly on my lips. He gently took off my top and leaned over my chest while my firm breasts were yearning to be loved by Chad. I felt so lose from the heat of his body wanting me. He made me desirous of him much more.

"Can you pose nude for me. I brought my camera along with me from Virginia, please." Chad implored.

I paused for a moment and compromised,

"Alright! But I want to have my bikini panties on. It does not take up all my flesh for your picture."

After the pictures were developed, the first person who complimented about how well the pictures were made was the technician that enlarged the nude pictures. Chad made the picture shots to capture my youthfulness. I thought to myself that — A Forever Young Me, Chad! His camera suspended the time of my youth. Because time takes its toll on our body and time is a killer on every one of us.

We went out for dinner then back to my place. While we looked at the album of my family pictures, the phone rang. Gus's voice was on the phone and he was at Hartsfield Airport. He came from California to see me.

I demonstrated,

"I have an old friend visiting me from Virginia. How could you do this to me, without calling me prior to your arrival?"

Gus Pleaded,

"April, I am your boyfriend. We had gone through so much together and I miss you very much. I will wait at the airport for an hour for you to get rid of your "old" friend."

Gus was peaceful and loving and known as a sharp man. By knowing him long before I knew how he felt to be rejected by me.

As I turned to Chad, he told me that he will leave because the distance from California is much father than the distance of Virginia. Chad was charming and gentle with me when he offered the way out for me.

When Gus arrived, it was eleven o'clock in the evening. He held me in his arms while my tears were falling from my eyes. I said,

"Gus, I can no longer do this with any man. I am torn between two loves. I am upset about my life. I wanted a simple life with one man. But not this way. You have power over me."

Gus comforted,

"When we get married, I want you to love me for what I am, not my physical attraction only, my heart and my feeling as well, even if it would take some time to build up our relationship."

After seeing Gus that time, I kept failing in health and was hospitalized for five years. Thus I lost all the contact with Gus, Chad and other friends. Then I met the man in red sneaker shoes who apparently became my mentor, my teacher and my hero in America. He fought many battles in my life for my honor and pride.

XVII

Gift of Satisfaction

He was standing at the corner of the Burger King near the bus stop. His right hand was holding the umbrella to avoid the rain. It was four o'clock on a Friday afternoon. He was wearing a light blue suit with red sneakers. The shoes are those that soccer players wear when they play ball. Rain continued to pour down. He was waiting for the bus. It looked like it was a prearranged happening that day and that hour. I went by where he was standing with the umbrella. In the rain I kept walking toward the liquor store to pick up a bottle of wine for the party at my girlfriend's home in East Point. I was waiting for the bus. He then approached me and offered his umbrella along with his friendly smile, I could not resist. I suggested that we share the umbrella. At last the bus arrived and the rain was abating. In the bus, I expressed my feelings,

"I am a one-man woman."

He replied,

"I am a one-woman man."

We became real friends from that moment on.

At the party of my girlfriend's home on Saturday evening, my girlfriend's husband, a band leader in the U.S. Army, had his friends, musicians and singles attend the party. Among those there was Fred, a friend of my girlfriend's husband. He was very sweet. Also John, another musician, was good company. And Bob, who was a warm fellow. They were all twenty-one or twenty-two years old. My girlfriend was making some snacks to add to our party while her husband was entertaining the guests. At the table I was sipping some wine and thinking of the guy I had met with the red sneakers. He looked as if he was one of the soccer champions in the Southeast Asian National Olympic team.

Fred's voice from the living room pulled my mind back to the party. He said,

"April, why are you so pensive? What are you thinking about?"

"Oh, no — I am sipping the wine and enjoying the burgundy flair."

"How do you like our party?" I asked.

The party went on until two o'clock the next morning. I could not stay up that late, so I went to bed an hour early and slept like a baby till noon.

The hero with the umbrella in the rain that day had been in my mind for a while. I crossed an intersection in town and as I was about to reach the other side, an auto driver lost control of the wheel and headed toward me. At the moment, I felt strong arms wrapped around me and fell down on the pavement while the out of control car continued rolling on the sidewalk ahead of us. I turned around and looked at the person that just saved my life. It was him, the man with the red sneakers.

Thereafter, we became the best of friends. I was his date every evening including weekends. When we got together, he always wore a different suit. He appeared to be rich and polite. He opened the door of his car for me every time. I always admired this tradition of American men. We went from the Burger King to a fine restaurant, and saw live night club shows together. We had a good time and he always took me home at the end of the evening. He was my hero.

"Once upon a time there was a great warrior, who survived a long life of many battles, and was able to keep his wealth the rest of his life. As the warrior grew older, his energy dwindled. When he stopped killing other men, that is when he lost his wealth." I said.

He asked,

"Will you illustrate your meaning of the story?"

I explained,

"When a man is falling in love with a beautiful woman inside and out, he is a warrior. His beautiful woman is his wealth and he protects his wealth at any price. In the battle of life, he has to defeat other men who come around with the intent to loot his "wealth." [2] When man stops struggling for survival, that is when he is growing old and when he loses his wealth."

I asked,

"How do you like my story?"

He did not look at the window anymore; he looked at me and held my hands in his hands. With a warm voice he said,

"April, you are very energetic. But I too have an energetic personality that probably matches yours or, perhaps, even exceeds yours."

He continued,

"Also, I know that I have the heart of a great warrior, and I have achieved my share of victories and suffered my share of scars in many battles. I know what it is to be battered and almost destroyed in the battles of life, but not defeated, for I am not defeated and never will be. I have been beaten to the ground,

[2] "Wealth" The beautiful woman of the man.

but I have arisen and I am arising, a wiser man, and I will never lose my wealth, even if I should happen to temporarily lose my money, because my wealth is in my spirit, my heart, and my mind — and I can always win back my money as long as my spirit never fails and I have the will and courage to fight and struggle. I have the heart of a champion. I am a winner; and I am determined to win."

"It is very impressive, please tell me more!" I said.

He went on,

"I am unafraid to fight and compete and struggle to win, but I am also unafraid to love; and I am kind, understanding, unselfish, loyal and loving. I am not weak, but I have surely learned that a man without love has no wealth, no matter how large his bank account and assets may happen to swell. But I am alone. I want to find a woman who understands and shares my life, ambitions, energy, and my spirit. I want her to understand my heart, and desires, and will walk beside me. Will it be you?"

I replied,

"You can write a good book! By the way, will you sing me a song, please? Music has enchanted my life and it gives me inspiration."

He replied,

"There is no beauty in my singing to the ears of those who hear it, I often sing and whistle and dance when I am alone myself."

I explained,

"But now you are not alone, you have me. Please sing a couple of fine tunes. I would be very happy to hear it."

And…, he did sing.

"When somebody loves you, it is no good unless she loves you, all the way — all the way."

Then, he asked me,

"Will you tell me a folk story of the orient?"

I asked him,

"What would you give me in return?"

He smiled and gently gave me a kiss on my cheek and said,

"Anything your heart desires."

I was exhilarated by what he said. The power of his words gave me a great fulfillment.

I started,

"The sound of the flute cut through the quiet evening from the river on the North side of the town. Its rhythm sent thrills to My Nương. In the palace home of her family, My Nương was seventeen and the only beloved child of a noble man.

One day, the sound of the flute on the river stopped. My Nương then felt ill and was in a serious condition. Her father learned about the reason of her illness. He then sent for the person who caused My Nương's state of health.

He was the ferry-man, who lived on the river, and made the flute sound in the evening. He was at the bedside of My Nương and started his flute. The melody of his flute had the power over My Nương's spirit. She rose up and smiled at her father, who had brought back the familiar sound of the flute. My Nương requested to see the man who had the talent she loved. Since the ferry-man was poor and ugly, he covered his face with a straw hat. My Nương demanded to see his face. By seeing his face, the ferry-man was able to witness the beauty of My Nương. By the same token, My Nương felt joy since the man with the flute was not what she thought: — "Prince Charming."

The ferry-man went home to his boat on the river. He felt ill. He was in love with My Nương the moment he saw her. The music of his flute was suspended for days. Then he died.

After he died, his grave had a shining glow visible especially at night. People from that town dug his grave up and found that the ferry-man's heart turned into a solid chunk of pink jade. Since the story of My Nương with the flute of the ferry-man had been known to the towns people, they then made a cup of tea from the ferry-man's heart (the pink jade) and sent it to My Nương as a gift of the ferry-man's heart.

My Nương sat in her room and enjoying her new cup of tea, which was a gift — a pink jade cup. As she sat looking at the tea in the cup, My Nương saw the ferry-man with his flute playing the familiar rhythm. My Nương then felt ill and died.

In the other world, My Nương and the ferry-man were able to live a life together side by side."

I continued,

"In conclusion, the ferry-man got My Nương's love and the music of his flute. But he does not look handsome. He was guilty of three charges:

He stopped to perform his flute and got his loved one ill, his look was one of murder, and his sin was being poor.

The moral of this story is that being poor is a sin."

XVIII

The Medicine Man

All the happy hours had ended. I went back to work in a local restaurant to pay my bills. I maintained well—balanced thoughts and a good spirit so I would not be down on myself. After trying so hard, I felt ill. The hero with the umbrella in his red sneakers understood my problems. He took me in his arms and comforted me with love and this was healing. Two months later, I was in ill health again. He then told me,

"What is a country? A country is a piece of land where everybody comes to live and helps to make it a country. After many generations, Vietnam is a rich cultural piece of land. Now, the United States is also a rich piece of land and this piece of land is the one you are in now."

Like My̆ Nương with the ferry-man in our oriental folk story I rose up and smiled with the world, here I am.

He said,

"Dear, you can make it. I believe you are going to make it."

He continued on,

"You are the only hope of the twenty-eight people in your family in Vietnam. You have got to get well and do it."

His words woke me up and I knew I must go on for the sake of my family in Vietnam. He was a medicine man. With the strength of his love, he healed all my hurtful moments that I had in my lifetime. He was the reason I felt alive.

* * *

I returned home tonight with a swollen toe in great pain. I soaked my foot in a bucket of warm water to ease the pain that was bothering me enormously. My friend walked in and saw my poor situation. He then got on the phone after finding out from me what had happened. He picked up the phone and called the restaurant. He said,

"My name is Stefan Bradley; I am a teacher at a high school in Chicago, Illinois. I need to talk to the manager of your restaurant."

A couple minutes later, the manager was on the phone. He said,

"Hello, may I help you?"

Stefan went on,

"I have a serious matter to discuss with you. What is your name, how tall are you, what is your weight?"

Stefan then said,

"I weigh two hundred twenty-five and I am six feet tall. I am a teacher. My friend, April, who is from the orient works in your restaurant, experienced an accident by your stepping on her foot. Where she came from, she would have a larger restaurant than yours. And believe me; this accident would have resulted in a severe reprimand of your carelessness. A wise decision on your part would have been to seek emergency medical attention which you did not. So you made two mistakes. Now I think that we should meet out in the parking lot on a friendly basis and see how your foot would feel with me dropping my foot on yours, no hard feelings except a sore foot for you. How would you like that my friend?"

The manager was obviously sorry for his mistake. He made it clear and he said,

"Mr. Bradley, I am very sorry about the accident. Please tell your friend to come back for medical attention, and it would certainly be a sore foot for me. And for you to write the district manager would be something I hope would not happen."

Stefan was very honest and straight. He lived his own way of life and did not have to be under other's supervision. I always liked Stefan and his sense of humor which was very refreshing. He did not speak vulgar but got right to the point and sometimes he used slang terms instead. He never wronged others. He stuck to whatever he made up his mind about. He was my friend, my bodyguard, and my hero. He was the man with the umbrella in the rain.

XIX

Dream of New Vietnam

The New Vietnam Restaurant had been in the business for more than a year. I usually went there when they had special dishes like Vietnamese home cooked foods such as "Chã Gìo" (a Vietnamese egg roll style), or "Bánh Xèo" (oriental pancake) and French coffee. I also enjoyed the company of the owners. They used to tease me about not having a family of my own. One of the owners asked me,

"Look around, the suitors are waiting for you and I am one of them."

He made me laugh and forget my headache that I had earlier from overworking the last two days. I told him that I would marry a Vietnamese man when I become real rich and famous, so we could come home to our family and we could be proud of ourselves with our relatives and friends because we made it. This made him satisfied. He was a little curious why I was not seen with anyone but an American Yankee from Chicago. He said,

"You like American men."

I made it sound like an excuse, I said,

"I had stewed fish too many days and I got sick of it. Americans were also sick and tired of their everyday hamburger. But, that is all they have. You can ask them."

He listened and seemed to be absorbed with my controversies. He threw at me a luscious look, and stated,

"In that case, I suggest that you would have multi-dishes of fish, fried fish, steamed fish, charcoal fish, grilled fish, broiled fish, etc., as a substitution of stewed fish. How about that? Aren't Vietnamese men better?"

Now I really got a red face. I insisted that I would have an American hamburger instead of fish everyday. I compromised with him,

"From now on I will call you fish, and we are all fish, okay"

259

I then illustrated,

"Fish live in the water (in Vietnamese water also means a country, nation, or state). We must have a country. Now, you tell me which country are we in?"

He gave me a knocked-out statement,

"Do not get married. If you get married, you will have only one man to love you. But if you do not get married, many men will love you."

I snapped the words from his mouth,

"…and you are one of the men?"

I made a statement, which sounded like I was giving him the opportunity for later. I said,

"My list was full, but I will see if I can fit you in."

He approached close to my table and asked me,

"My friend, I bet you that I could finish my big glass of coke before you even drink your cup of tea."

He went on,

"...with one condition that you do not touch my glass."

I looked at him with wonderment,

"Are you sure you know what you are talking about?"

Following my question, he said,

"Look!"

He took the bigger empty glass upside-down over my small cup of tea. Then he knocked off the glass of coke which was already on the table while I and others were staring at him in amazement. He was my fellow country man, my neighbor, who was so amusing.

Another time, I walked into the restaurant in sport clothes. The same hilarious friend the owner, told me,

"You are wearing the same clothes for two days. Why don't you wear something else so I can look at you?"

I responded quickly,

"When you love someone, even in her birthday suit, you still love her. Don't you?"

He yelled with excitement,

"You are right, I love it!"

I located a table by the entrance. A waitress took my order and went back to the kitchen. A few minutes later she came back with the beef noodle soup on her tray. I ate it all. The owner was watching me. He commented,

"You eat too fast. That is not good for you."

I responded,

"Actually, I was not hungry. I just came here to see you. If I get sick from eating too much, you will end up paying my doctors bill."

"Sure, I will even buy life insurance for you if I am the beneficiary," He laughed with elation thinking that he has defeated me.

I told him,

"You are too much of an American yourself and you have learned too quickly the American ways."

"You are too much of an American yourself too," he said.

In Vietnam there is no life insurance.

XX

Zero Hour

Zero was my neighbor next door. He came from Cuba and had been in the United States for more than twenty years. His wife also was from Cuba. He was seventy-three and his wife was sixty- five years old. Every day Zero was working on their flower garden in the back yard of their home. I had to run some errands and asked Zero if he would come along to give me a hand.

We walked in a local restaurant and saw a number of friends who were drinking beers together. We sat down at their table and ordered two cups of coffee. Barry, one of those in the group, whispered in my ear,

"He is too old. What can he do for you?"

I told Barry, that in the Orient, people feel differently about age. The older is better. We should show some respect to our elderly people because we are all going to be there soon. This made Barry more jealous of Zero. He said,

"April, if you need me just tell me. You do not have to take the old man out with you I have been waiting to move in with you and be your roommate for two hundred and fifty dollars a month."

"Barry, I do not need a roommate now. If I do just remember two hundred and fifty dollars a month rent does not include me, only your own private room and the use of the kitchen. You sleep in your room and I sleep in my room. That is it. There is no such thing as renting a room and a roommate all together for one price. You must be out of your mind to think that I would let you move in."

I asked the waiter to bring five beers for five of my friends. It was my treat. They were very impressed with my generosity. They kept telling me what a nice lady I am. These people, who I called my friends, never knew where I lived and I never knew where they lived either. We met in restaurants, shops, or markets every now and then. I looked at Zero, my neighbor, as my father. But in the eyes of my American friends, Zero was my boyfriend.

One day my loving American boyfriend got mad at Zero because I was giving him too much attention. He condemned Zero as a taker. My boyfriend was thinking of how the old Cuban man got so much of my attention. He did not understand that a five thousand year-old culture had formed my thinking about the old man. I am sure the culture of Cuba is not much different. Americans in the United States, who have never been abroad, do not understand these cultures.

While in the restaurant, I turned around and saw Pete at the other table. He made a gesture that he wanted to talk to me. I waved my hand at him and asked him to come over to our table.

Pete was Belgian. He was very husky amongst the group in the restaurant. He pulled his chair close to me and said,

"Do not worry about Barry. He is just a typical American man. America is beautiful, but a man like him makes life difficult."

I protested,

"American men are gorgeous!"

"April, try Belgian men, you will love it. Nobody in the world plays football but Americans. Everybody else plays soccer." he chucked.

I glanced at Pete,

"I have a boyfriend."

Pete did not give up. He said,

"I am a better man."

"That is okay with me. If Barry is typical, I can always teach him not to be typical. When you love someone, you are willing to do many things for your loved one. In this case, Barry and I are just friends. I can only do so much for him, but I bought him a beer. Zero came along to keep me company. He left Castro, the Communist in Cuba, just as many others from the

267

Indochina War have left for freedom. They all paid a very high price to be in the United States. That person left home for one reason only, and that was for their freedom."

"Whose theory of the Communist?"

Carlos from Chile asked,

"Lenin's theory from the Soviet Union." I replied.

I explained,

"Therefore, Lenin's theory may not be all bad. It has a different government system from the free world. Its government controls the people in their everyday life. Here, we have the freedom to vote and our government is by people's choice, and free enterprise is what the Communist government does not have. However, it is a very complicated discussion. There is one thing I know that Lenin's theory could spread out to the whole world in some time later, not in our generation, but it will come. One way or another, to avoid the Third World War with nuclear and nerve gas, which will destroy the earth. I think we ought to know which way to go from here, and to make wise decisions for our generation and the generations that follow."

Zero and I shook hands and then said goodbye to our friends. We will see them again some other time. That was the end of our visit at the restaurant. Zero said,

"April, you are very generous and sharp. I am very proud of you. I will tell all my friends of how wonderful you are and let me know if there is anything I can do for you."

I said,

"Zero, you need to buckle up your seat belt before we hit the road? The cops in Atlanta are on the streets giving tickets."

Another time, my friend, who wore red sneaker shoes and I sat down at the table of all seven Vietnamese fellow countrymen. We ate and talked a while. One Vietnamese man asked me why I had an American boyfriend but not a Vietnamese man. I translated to my American friend what the Vietnamese man said. My friend with red sneaker shoes got off his chair to kneel on the floor. He picked my foot up in his hand

and kissed it. He then asked me to translate to the Vietnamese men at the table if they can do that. Of course, no one would. My red sneaker shoe friend is very highly intelligent. It helped me greatly to satisfy the inquisitive mind of my fellow countrymen. There are bad, good and different people in our lifetime. My American friend is definitely the better one. I said to my red sneaker shoe friend,

"When you are around, there is a second best."

XXI

The Strength of Youth

During my childhood, when I was twelve, I always had my brothers as chaperones for me to and from home to school. My younger brother was three years younger than I. One afternoon while leaving the school, three school boys came after me and one of the boys grasped my hand to tell me that he had a crush on me. My younger brother saw all that. He escorted me home and changed his clothes to go combat the school boys that evening.

The custom in the orient is that family girls hold their personal pride very high. Girls were taught to be decent and moral. By being decent means a lady does not hang out with boys in the streets, or even the restaurants. If they are serious, they must go to see her family and make a formal recognition of who they are. When they have met this formality, they then are allowed to visit their sweetheart at home with her parents,

271

brothers, or sisters present. Boys, who were not serious, would not come around and follow this custom.

My younger brother felt that the school boys hurt my dignity. In the open field, he met the other boys. He said,

"I am only myself and can only see one of you at a time."

One of the boys told him,

"Sởn is my classmate, a good boy. He just wanted to hold the hand of your sister. Why do you want to make it a big deal? We three can beat you."

My younger brother said,

"That is right, you beast! You only wanted to hold her hand in public. That is why you boys have to pay and the price is right. She was not there for you boys to play games with. Go home and play with your own sister."

The boys were furious with him. They began to confront him one by one. My younger brother knew some karate from our cousin, who had a black belt in karate and was judo instructor for the national police headquarters. The boys were a couple of years older than he. But they did not know how to fight. After an hour of battle, the boys left, and my younger brother arrived home at ten o'clock that night. His clothes were all shredded. He told me what happened and he said the boys will not do that to me anymore. I went to school next day and everything was peaceful. My younger brother was my bodyguard and my hero.

My second older brother was a quiet person. In school he was always the first or the second student in the class grading. When he was in a good mood, he might say a couple of words. Other than that, he was very tranquil and minded his own business. When he was seventeen, he graduated from a radio technical school. He could build his own radio from pieces.

As usual, he came from school on his bike in the evening. The boy of a distant neighborhood stopped him on the way and wanted his bike. He was alone and fought with others. He got hurt plus he lost his shirt, too. Two days later, he somehow managed to get his bike back and left a big cut on the forehead of the other boy. His mother came to our home and claimed that our older brother hurt her son. Our mother told them that their son had battered our brother a couple of days ago and we did not complain about that. So, why did she come to complain about this?

My older brother was always kind to me. When I was five, he used to carry me on his back to candy stores, and waited there until I was through with my shopping. He was my chaperon, my bodyguard.

When I was five, my parents had a live-in maid and also a nanny. Next to our mother was our oldest brother. They were the two people in the house that I was comfortable with. I did not like our nanny. But if our mother was not around, my oldest brother took care of me instead of the nanny.

One afternoon, my oldest brother took me in his arms and told me to keep quiet because father was sleeping. We are going to the mango and blueberry trees garden, and he would get all the fruits for me. When we arrived at the big blueberry trees, he sat me down beneath them and he climbed up a tree and filled his hat with blueberries. When he stood on the ground, he gave me his hat with blueberries and said,

"All these blueberries are yours. Promise me that you are not going to tell father that I did this. If he finds out he will punish me. I did it for you, okay sweetheart?"

My brother pulled out of his shirt a package of cigarettes, and began to smoke them. I had a mouthful of blueberries and I told him,

"You told me not to tell our father about you climbing up the tree, but what about you smoking cigarettes? Father does not want you to smoke either."

My brother dropped the cigarette in his hand, he said,

"This includes the cigarette smoking. Do not tell father also. You see, I risked my life to get you the blueberries. So take your time — do not eat in a hurry like that, it is all yours."

Then, I quit eating my blueberries. I was mad at my brother who just did the best for me. I told him,

"Brother, you have insulted me. I eat any way I want because you told me that these are my blueberries. Now you

275

are telling me how bad I ate them. I am telling you now that our father will learn about what you have done all this afternoon."

My poor brother was visibly shaking by my threat of exposure. He was asking me to forget about what he said. He promised not to say anything like that again. I was still hurt from what he said, and I had made up my mind that father was going to hear about this.

Our father was up. He asked us where we had been. Our mother was there in the living room to protect my brother. He told her about us earlier. I began telling him,

"We went out to the mango and blueberry tree garden. Brother went up the tree and got me some blueberries."

Our mother snapped at me,

"She is lying. He did not climb up the tree. Do not listen to her."

I stood at the corner of the living room and almost started crying, I said,

"Father, look at my tongue. It is still black from eating the blueberries in the field."

That evening, my brother received a severe punishment from father. I saw all that and was feeling bad because of the betrayal for what I had done to my brother. Until these days when I think of it, I just want to cry. He was my chaperon, he was my bodyguard, but I turned him in.

A week later, I walked along the river bank to find my older brother for my mother. He was swimming with other kids in the river near by our home. While I was walking, I was thinking of putting a paper bag on my head, which my mother gave me before I left the house. I was only five years old and thought I would have fun with the paper bag my mother gave me to carry some fish. I thought I would try walking with the paper bag over my face and see if I could walk anyway — but I fell in the river. Luckily, the water in the river was low and my brother saw me. He ran and jumped in the water to rescue me. He held me in his arms and shook me to make sure that I was not unconscious. I opened my eyes and looked at my dear old brother and with much love for his saving me. He scolded me and said,

"You have scared me to death. I thought you were drowning and I thought you drank all the water in the river. God has punished you for telling father to be hard on me."

The reason he was mad at me was because of the blueberries he gathered for me from the forbidden tree. I told our father about him climbing in the tree to pick the blueberries. My father had forbid my brother from doing that. I guess my brother had a good reason to be angry with me. My father severely punished him for not following his orders.

I felt a pain in my chest, so I asked my old brother to forgive me. I was too much of a child when I did that to him. My older brother forgave me and after that I never caused him any trouble with our father.

When I was twelve years old, my father was stationed in a military training zone. Our family's home was amongst the fine officers homes in that area. The military post was for all the family of officers similar to my father. My father was a Major. His military duties included being in charge of that post.

Our home was the meeting place for all the kids on the block. They came to study or to play with me and my brothers. My mother was very sociable and she loved kids. She was a gospel preacher for Cao Dai religion. This is a form of Buddhism, and we were members of the temple. Therefore, our friends and neighbors often came to our home to study religious writings. Cao Dai religion is based on the many philosophies of Buddhism, Confucianism and Christianity. My mother had many friends throughout South Vietnam. Not only because of her religious leadership but she also performed cataract surgery.

Every time during recess at school, I went to the soft drink stand. A young woman, who owned the stand, usually waited on me. I made friends with her and knew where she lived. She lived with her two small children. They lost the father in battle. She was selling soft drinks to take care of her two small children. I asked her if I could come to her home one weekend. She said,

"Sure, if you want to visit me, but my home is very poor. We have only a couple chairs in the whole house."

The weekend came and I was at her door. A young boy, who was approximately eight years old, greeted me at the door. He had a younger sister approximately four or five years old. The boy told me that his mother should be home anytime soon. When their mother arrived, she was coughing continuously with her shoulders dropped down to her body. Blood came out from her mouth. After a few minutes, I waited there. The mother and the small children told me that she had tuberculosis and had no money to go see a doctor. If she had to quit her work one day her two small children would not have anything to eat that day. She stated that her tuberculosis was contagious and they had no other relatives that her kids could stay with. They had all died in the war.

I went home and broke my piggy bank and shook out all my savings. I then gave it all to her, which amounted to about twenty dollars. This was not enough for her to go see a doctor and buy medicine. I broke the rule of not stealing to help her. I went out of my way to help the family, especially the mother, who was dying of tuberculosis. I cut the barbwire around the military post, which was within my father's jurisdiction, which averaged ten kilos per day. In ten days I gathered one hundred kilos. Each kilo sold for fifty cents, which meant I accumulated fifty dollars. Thus, my dear friend, the mother was able to get herself to see a doctor and buy some medicine for her tuberculosis. The taking of the barbwire left the fence with a large opening of nearly one tenth of a mile. This was, of course, quite obvious. On the last day that I cut the barbwire, I fell on a triangle bar, which was about fifteen inches above the ground. My leg caught a deep cut about two inches below my right knee. Blood profusely gushed down my leg. I ripped my blouse sleeve off to wrap around my knee. I rushed to a local pharmacy to get emergency first aid. After getting emergency first aid, I went back to safely conceal the barbwire when my knee felt better. In a day or two, I went back to retrieve the hidden barbwire.

That night, my father came home with a stern look. He could not understand why the barbwire of the fence in the post was missing, leaving a big gap. He said,

"Nobody would dare to do this, except somebody who lives here on the post," my father murmured to himself.

I was worried that my father would find out that I did it because of the cut on my knee. So I made up an excuse that I was not feeling too well so I could stay out of his sight. My father always gave me special loving attention because I was his only girl. My four brothers were well aware of that. Nevertheless, my father was severe with all of us, if any of us did wrong. I had no choice; I had to help my friend. What I did was so serious that it could jeopardize my father's high standing.

Because of the cut on my knee, I acquired a high fever. The next day my mother noticed my poor physical condition. She rushed me to the hospital for emergency treatment. It took me a couple of months to regain my health and save my life and keep from loosing my leg.

My mother was a very articulate lady. Most of everything she did for her children was based on the Buddhist teachings. She said,

"You are a child of a religious family, but you got in trouble by stealing the fence from government property. The reason you got hurt was the price you had to pay." my mother explained.

I said,

"I did not want my friend, the mother of the two small children, to die because of no medicine."

My mother instructed me,

"You could have told me and we could have done something together."

I explained,

"The cost for my friend to see a doctor was a lot of money. The only way I thought I could get the money for her to see a doctor was to get and sell the barbwire. Altogether, I sold about one hundred kilos for fifty dollars, mother."

My mother said,

"When your father asks you about your knees, just tell him that you fell on your knee on the steel bar. If he is not satisfied then tell him that you fell on the barbwire fence on the post. He will not ask you any more after that. I will cover for you somehow. But, if worst comes to worst, just tell him that the reason you did it was to help a friend. I think he will not be too upset with you."

That night when I got home, my father's anger was enormous. I never saw him that angry. The roof of our home could have come down by his loud hollering. After a few moments he calmed down and asked me to explain my actions. When he learned why I did it, he cried,

"You have got that from your mother. Even though I am a soldier, I never killed anyone. My job is mostly in the training field. I train the soldiers how to fight in battle. If I had to kill, I would kill. You have a heart of a preacher, which is your mothers and a spirit of a soldier, which is from me. You could have gotten killed because there are mines in between the barbwire fences. You had to have guts to do that. Just promise me that next time you will not haul all off the military supplies on the post." My father remarked.

This showed the depth of my father's feelings for his only daughter. In that way my father's justice had been done. For our family, whenever disputes took place amongst us, he always made the final decisions in the household. My dispute between my mother and my father usually lasted only until they covered the subject to exhaustion. They used history to prove their points. My father stated,

"The King of the Great Wall in China would have been a great King, if it was not because of a seductive, magical and lustful Queen that he was married to."

My mother's voice replied defensively to my father,

"If it was not because of the King being overly sexed, hooked on booze and beautiful women, the King would have been able to save his country."

Their dispute had brought to me and my brothers a valuable educational background in that regards.

I joked with my mother,

"Oh! The great old China had made a wine head, their King, eh!"

My mother replied,

"Yes, anyone who drinks day and night like that could become a King of wine heads."

XXII

Teacher Knows Best

My high school was owned by a Catholic family. The principal was a father of a large Catholic church. He had three nephews who were history, mathematics, and biology teachers. They were very good looking and unmarried. Dzong was my favorite history teacher. He smiled with everyone all the time. But when it came to study he was very grim.

Teachers in the orient are highly respected. They set a good example, and they are admired by everyone. Three times a week our sixty students in the classroom would meet for history. One time, after an hour of history class, everyone had a fifteen minute break. During the break period, the teacher normally asked all students to remain in the classroom for special stories. Dzong started,

"Once upon a time there was an international art contest with all the countries in the world competing. Each artist represented their country and they all met together at one place in a large auditorium. The speaker started the proceeding with the following,

"Ladies and gentlemen, this is a contest of one hundred fifty countries of the world and each artist has five minutes to paint a picture with a story to go along with it. Each minute there will be a bell ringing, thank you and good luck."

The bell rang and the contest began. All artists commenced with their paintings, except for one artist who was busy lighting up his cigar. The audience was bewildered as to why that artist did not immediately start his painting. The bell rang at the second minute and then the artist finished his cigar. This time someone in the audience loudly said,

"He must be crazy! Which country sent him here?"

The bell rang at the third minute. Now the artist began to empty his bag and took out an electric paint sprayer and a canvas. The bell rang on the fourth minute. This time the audience was actually agitated with the artist who had not done the painting and all he had was one more minute and then the contest would end. So with the last minute left he sprayed black paint on the canvas. It was a beautiful and shining black board on his canvas. The bell rang at the fifth minute. Each artist started to explain the story of their painting. Some artists finished with a good painting job but time ran out too quickly so they did not have time to work on their story. Some others did have the stories for their paintings but their paintings were not completed. So they were disqualified. Now the artist who painted a beautiful black board announced the meaning and story of his painting. He said,

"Ladies and gentlemen, this black board represents a love story of two black lovers in a black night."

The audience applauded the artist who had completed a beautiful black story and of course he won the contest. Another artist standing next to him was angered for the easy job the artist had done. This artist dipped his brush in the white paint and made a dash on the beautiful black painting of the other artist. The audience cried out loud that the beautiful painted picture was destroyed and there was no more meaning to it now. The artist who had won the contest gently announced the explanation of his painting,

"Ladies and gentlemen, the love story of the black lovers in the dark night has not finished. After satisfying each other one of them smiled."

Hands clapped all over the auditorium and voices from everywhere shouted "Bravo!"

Teacher Dzong explained,

"Do not be afraid to be different from others. The artist who had won the contest was the different one. He had a good reason to be different. In another words, he was exceptionally special."

I and others in the classroom rose up to Dzong's desk for his autograph. He was an author of all his own stories. He did it very well and we all admired him.

Dzong was a loving idol to the school girls in the class. Many girls tried to catch his attention in varied ways. They dressed up with nail polish and make up every day. Everyone, that is, except me! My mother told me to dress casual, not in style and absolutely no make up. She had good reason for me to do so. Her reason was to keep me out of trouble with the boys in the school. My mother always seemed to know best.

Dzong kept cool with everyone, until one afternoon while I was in the class. The Catholic father went to visit my parents in regards to my marrying Dzong, my history teacher. My parents told father that they will talk it over with me and will let father know soon.

Mother asked me,

"Do you know you are a grown up girl now? Soon you will be married and have your own family. You will leave me and your father for your husband."

I protested,

"Mom, are you kidding? I grew up in this family all my life. I will live here with you forever. I will not have a husband."

My mother inquired,

"How do you like Dzong, your history teacher? I have heard that he is a good man, and very handsome."

I said, innocuously,

"I like his stories in the class. He has a great sense of humor."

My mother continued,

"Would you marry him? His uncle came here this afternoon to ask us if you would marry his nephew, Dzong."

"Mother, I do not know what love is. I only know one love. That is my love for dad, you, and my brothers. I do not need a husband. Besides, I am happy in our family home," I replied.

XXIII

Almost a Hollywood Star

When I turned fourteen, I worked with my school band singing songs and participated in school plays. I performed often, especially at the end of the year around school graduation festivities. I was also deeply involved with the helping of the South Vietnam Army band. The military band leader, Greg, met me and gave me a proposition of singing with the band. Due to the fact I was still in school, I only worked on Friday, Saturday and Sunday nights with the Army band. I sang for the National Military Training School called The Quang Trung Training Center. Quang Trung was the title of King Nguyễn Huệ. The King had swept out all the trouble of the nation and pushed back the Chinese invaders in those old days, according to history.

The first time I appeared before about five thousand military trainees, I was very nervous. My Uncle Greg noticed my worry and he said to me,

"Do not worry, you will get used to it. Just look at the audience as though they are not there. Also, I am behind you to give you all the support you need,"

I went to the center of the stage and with the microphone in my hand, I started to sing. At the end of the song, I received a roar of applaud from the audience. A number of the people from the audience came to the back of the stage to give me flowers and their handkerchiefs, and to let me know that they liked me. From then on, I developed much confidence in my performances. My Uncle Greg was always supportive. He gave me all the necessary instructions a singer need to know.

After that, I gained greater success. I was welcomed by everyone and received many letters, flowers and beautiful postcards from many of the people from the audience.

The time came for my most exciting experience connected with the Twentieth Century Fox Movie Company from America, who joint ventured with the Vietnamese Alpha Motion Picture Company. They made a movie in my home town, called The Tiger Year. My two older brothers were hired as extras as guards to a scholar, who came home from afar. The Director with the Twentieth Century Fox Company had blue eyes-and blonde hair, was tall and husky and in his mid forties. He asked me where I lived, and he said he wanted to meet my family. The president of Alpha Motion Picture Company translated to me in English, since at that time I spoke very little English.

When the Director came to see our home, my parents were impressed with the man who had blue eyes and blonde hair. He gave my parents the proposition of bringing me to the United States of America to go to school and develop into the movie business. He said, he would advance one hundred thousand U.S. Dollars. My parents decided to decline the offer. My parents were very conservative Vietnamese. They practiced Buddhism and Confucianism philosophy and believed that money and wealth were only temporary goals – a belief not unlike that of the Christian faith. They believed in good humanitarian goals and a good life would result, and that is what counted. If I got into the movie business, they believed I would change husbands like changing shirts, which was not adhering to good Buddhist philosophy. Their wish was my command and they stuck to their older traditional ways of thinking of deep seated beliefs strongly connected with the fact that money did not mean everything.

After deciding not to go to Hollywood to be in the movie business, I worked with the Vietnamese military band. The band leader, whom my family and I called "Uncle," was in his early forties and was an excellent songwriter and also published many fine songs. His title was Greg. Every time the band crew would go somewhere for a performance, Uncle Greg would drive to my family's home to pick me up and drop me off and he always watched over me. One afternoon, Uncle Greg confided in me about his marital difficulties. He told me that his wife was overly jealous. He said she accused him of unfaithfulness to her,

"You travel too much and must have somebody else."

Therefore, Uncle Greg said,

"Must I commit suicide because my wife is driving me insane?"

Uncle Greg and his family fled to Saigon from Hanoi back in 1954. He told me that the government of Hanoi was extremely harsh and that resulted in his leaving the North. He told me that after his death, I should not continue in the singing profession. He said,

"A singing career is one of the worst existences. If the drummer was unsatisfied with no sex from me, he would beat the wrong rhythm. If the lead guitar man did not have me, he would play the wrong melody and thus more problems."

I would have to sleep with everyone. An attractive up and coming new female vocalist would have all these problems to face. Uncle Greg had explained to me about some common problems of a singing career for the many female singers and their struggle to become top vocalist. Uncle Greg said,

"You are a lovely young lady from a fine family and you have got to be able to do something else. Something which does not blemish your family's integrity and your own."

Three weeks later, Uncle Greg critically shot himself in his office. He had left a wife and two small children behind. He was my teacher and sweet Uncle and for years I felt saddened because of his self inflicted death.

Uncle Greg's death brought much grief to the musicians and performers. He should have left his wife and started a new life and find new happiness. He took his life due to the stupid idea that divorce in Vietnam was unthinkable. Suicide back then was a more common alternative for some Vietnamese. But of course, from the American viewpoint — divorce is the acceptable solution.

XXIV

The Luck We Shared / Deception

Our International Restaurant with live stage productions was celebrating its first year in business. Government consuls and high officials from many nations had been dining in our restaurant. Therefore, I had many enjoyable opportunities to get acquainted with these very sophisticated people. I kept a low profile and managed our business in a way that the Internal Revenue Service and other government authorities would not interfere too much. Adriane, Chan, and I were a company of three owners.

Claude, who was twenty-three years old, was the Director of the Denise Frere Trading Company. He arrived in Saigon from Paris one year previously and worked in the Saigon office for two years. I can still see him sitting around a large round table with his colleagues and drinking French champagne.

Every Friday, Claude came and ate dinner or lunch at our dinner club. One day I asked him,

"Claude, it is interesting that you have been eating here on Fridays regularly. But why don't you eat meat on Fridays?"

Claude replied,

"First of all, I am a Catholic; we do not eat meat on Fridays. It happens that your restaurant cooks the most delicious western omelets for lunch and crème-de-vollaide for dinner with your French bread. Second, I admire you as a young and beautiful proprietor of this grand place. Some Frenchmen maybe are chauvinists, but when it comes to women, "Cest L'armour Vive La France" If you want France, I will make a gift of it to you — I promise."

I responded,

"Claude, you talk like King Louis de Fourteenth of France. He was a playboy."

His sense of humor was strong, so he replied,

"King Louis de Fourteenth of France was an old man. I am King Louis de Twenty-third of France, and I do not eat meat on Fridays. Believe me; everything I said to you was with clear sanity."

Three months passed by, and Claude continued on a regular basis to eat with us on Fridays. But this day was Wednesday and he walked in and looked for me. Claude inquired,

"I have created a new business with my company, and we need a seafood and kapok supplier in town to export it to France, Italy, Brazil and Belgium. All of the buyers will be dealing in cash as the deliveries arrive at the docks in Saigon. I want to give this business to you, so you can do it as a side line to make extra money. Can we have a candle light dinner for us tomorrow evening at the Continental Palace?"

I replied,

"Claude, I do not have much time. Between the restaurant business and CEDEFEXCO (Asia Bicycle Manufacturing, Inc.),

I spent almost all my day with these businesses. However, my younger brother might want to do this. Give me a few days to check with him and I will get back with you. Anyhow, I will be very happy to have dinner with you."

After the dinner at the Continental Palace, Claude invited me to have dinner at his home the following Monday.

At the door, Claude stood and greeted me with a smile, he said,

"Hello darling! I was waiting for you and you are so punctual:"

I stated,

"Being punctual is good business practice and it is good self discipline."

I gave Claude a grin and walked in. His living room was so artistic in modern Spanish motif with white walls, a white group sofa with lots of windows and absolutely the whole place was spotless. The red tile on the floor in the living room contrasted with the white walls, giving the room an exquisite look of a

Western-European atmosphere. In the middle of the living room was a polar bear carpet. With admiration, I sat down comfortably with Claude and praised his place with,

"You have a beautiful setup here, Claude."

Claude responded,

"It is not as beautiful as your smile with those sexy lips of yours."

Frenchmen have been known to be the greatest lovers of all time as well as very cultured. I stated,

"You make me feel very flattered. Are all Frenchmen like you?"

With serenity, Claude explained,

"The average Frenchman knows how to talk to a lady. Napoleon won many battles for France. It is in the world history books. As much as our Frenchmen likewise fight the battles to win over their lady's hearts, the Frenchmen do things with pride and honor but they do not compete with each other like the American men."

Claude knew that in my profession as a proprietor of a first class night club and show bar restaurant. I dealt with a number of American high officials. He was very bright to make this statement and I said approvingly,

"Frenchmen have won the hearts of millions such as Mr. Victor Hugo and Alexander Rose who had invented the Vietnamese language and their French culture greatly influenced Vietnamese civilization."

"Just what I thought! You are perfect, my darling! You are educated and there is always some good in this world and you have been raised with many of the fine qualities of a high level Vietnamese family. I have lots of respect for you and your family," Claude explained with pleasure.

I answered,

"My parents are firm believers of God and Confucianism. They believe that the French civilization had brought their fine cultural traditions to the Vietnamese. They were proud of the events of the French founders of the Vietnamese written language."

Claude suggested,

"So, could this Frenchman get you something to drink?"

"I prefer Perrier Water, do you have it?" I said.

Claude replied enthusiastically,

"Sure, would you like some French music?"

Claude placed a tape in the tape deck and the sweet soft melody began. Claude leaned over and gave me a kiss on my ear and towards my lips. He then wrapped his arm around my waist and with the other held my hand lifted me up in a standing position so that he could lead my body close to his. Claude was so charming even when he was silent. He had a magnetic charm of modern man in the twentieth century. His eyes were shining as though he could see through my soul and his face was glowing. I liked him very much. I also liked Paul, his associate, who also was the Director of imports from France. They made me the offer of the possibility of my exporting seafood and kapok with Denise Frere Trading Company, a one hundred years old trading company in Saigon. Claude was handsome and slim. He had a shot of Benedictine and his eyes did not leave me for a second. He held me in his arms tenderly and danced with me. Claude asked me,

"Would you like to shampoo my hair? Have you ever done that with anyone before?"

"No, I have not done that before. But I will do it for you. Claude, you have the look of the French actor Alan Delon, a sex symbol in France." I answered.

With a cordial way, Claude warmly said,

"Do I appeal to you? That is important to me!"

I replied,

"You do appeal to me and you just did not know."

Claude released his arms from me and took off his shirt and then went straight to the bathroom — I followed him. In a seductive manner, he undressed himself. He stepped into the bathtub and turned the water on. I pulled a chair next to the

306

bathtub, which was already there and sat down on the edge and I started shampooing his hair. Claude said,

"I like your soft fingers rubbing on my scalp and it makes me so relaxed."

"Thank you, just enjoy it." I said.

Five minutes passed and Claude asked me,

"Will you rinse my hair?"

I replied,

"Certainly!"

I sat still on the chair while Claude finished with his bath. Claude got out of the bathtub and walked over to the towel hanger. When he climbed out of the bathtub, I viewed his full frontal naked body. He was magnificent, what a man! He stirred me wildly.

Claude said enticingly,

"In a few minutes, we are going to eat dinner together. My cook has fixed something very special for you this evening. For an appetizer, fresh stuffed tomatoes with tenderloin pork and salmon; and for desert, Baked Alaska. Would you care for some French wine, darling?"

I replied,

"Sure, I will have a glass of wine with you. You are an excellent host, Claude."

Claude expressed,

"Just for you! All I want to do is to be with you as often as possible and you can tell me anything that is on your mind."

I said,

"Claude, I can sing."

Claude looked at me without a blinking of his eyes, said,

"My darling can sing? April, you are an amazing lady. The more I know about you, the more I like you."

I continued,

"I can also paint watercolor portraits, figures, objects or animals. You have offered me France as a gift; now it is my turn to give you something in return — a song, my handsome man of mine,"

"J'ai quitté mon pays

J'ai quitté mon amie. J'ai quitté ma masion.

Ma vie, ma triste vie de trainer sans raison.

Solel Solei de mon pays perdu, de ville blanche que j'amais

regard, je dis, adieur."

In English, this song means:

"I left my country

I left my friend. I left my house

My life, my sad life.

Oh Sun, Oh Sun of my country is afar. The white town which

I may never see it again, I said, goodbye."

I dropped in the wing chair and said,

"I am sorry. I can not sing the rest of the song, because it is so sad. It is about leaving home and never seeing it again."

Claude gently said,

"You sing very well. When you sing you did not even have an accent. I enjoyed your song and it is my honor to be your exclusive audience. Did you write the song?"

I smiled and responded,

"It is a masterpiece song that I learned when going to French school in Saigon."

I did not realize until years later after I left Vietnam, that the song still brought tears to my eyes for many years.

There after, we became one. Claude was always sweet and decent with me. He took me to dinner and parties and sometime his associate, Paul, went with us.

Adriane was my best girl friend and also my business partner of Asia Bicycle Manufacturer of CEDEFEXCO in Saigon. She was twenty-three and was a young beautiful blossom. She could pick almost any man in Saigon. But she unfortunately was attracted to Claude. Her reasons were his business connections. However, I trusted Adriane enough to invite her to Claude's home for a cocktail party. I had never had any suspicion of our friendship and her respect for my relationship with Claude. After the experience of my friendship with Adriane and until this day, I am always cautious and have a watchful eye of suspicion of her intention both personal and business. I have resisted the feeling that she wanted to betray me.

I dropped in to be with Claude at his home at an unexpected time. Claude greeted me at the door and invited me in. Adriane was there. Claude explained to me that Adriane just came unexpectedly to visit and nothing had happened between them. He had not expected her to come by. Claude came and sat beside me and held my hand in his hand. Frenchmen are sophisticated lovers. He knew how much better I would feel if he could show me that he cared and Adriane's visit was innocent in his eyes. I turned to Adriane in a serious but loving way and said,

"Why did you come here when you knew I was not here?" In an awkward approach, Adriane said,

"I just dropped in because I thought you were here."

But she had not convinced me of her innocence. Obviously, she did not come to Claude's home to look for me. She just made that up to protect herself from me knowing her real intentions. I merely let this incident slide without embarrassing Adriane in front of Claude. So I said with a smile and love in my heart,

"Look, but hands off. He is my private property and do not go after him. The seafood and kapok business is already under my direction and control. We should not allow this to get between us."

After listening to my statement, Adriane made an excuse to leave the premises. Claude told me that Adriane wanted the business proposition to be hers. I asked Claude in an inquisitive mode,

"Do you want Adriane to have my seafood and kapok enterprise?"

In a tranquil voice, he said,

"The business belongs to April and is totally and completely your own - not Adriane's. She came with the intention of getting me to give her the business. I would rather have a beautiful woman that is good at heart and true, than have a woman full of traitorous intentions. What made Adriane think that she has such a power over me or over you?"

Claude continued,

"My sweetheart, I would like to share something important with you. It is not your enemies, which are far away, that you should worry about, but it is your questionable friends which act close to you that could do you harm. In this case, you are the one that I have chosen and I trust and love you fully."

Three months before my departure to the United States, I met Claude at his home. Claude told me to come to France with him and we would get married in France. Claude said,

"April, you come to France with me. I will take care of everything for you. There is nothing here in Saigon for an industrious person like you because in the next few months people here will have to experience painful changes in their life and in government. I can not leave you here, darling."

I explained,

"Claude, first I have got to make some arrangements for my family to remain here with security. What I mean is to give them all the rights for access to my bank accounts and businesses. Give me a couple weeks to do that."

Claude reassured me,

"Please do not change your mind not to go to France with me. I will wait for you."

XXV

Fate Will Tell

I arrived at my CEDEFEXCO office at fifteen past eight to make an arrangement with the shipment of fifty bicycles. They were for Vietnamese government purchases. Paul walked in and said solemnly,

"Bad news!"

Paul continued on,

"April, this is not easy for me to break the bad news to you. Early this morning Claude died from a rocket shell that hit his home while he was sleeping. A piece of shrapnel pierced his head. He apparently died instantly. His funeral will take place this evening but his body will be shipped to France. We all felt so sad."

When I heard that Claude was dead, I could not believe it. I was in a state of shock. I stared at Paul and with tears in my eyes slowly reacted in an extremely horrified state of mind. I said,

"No, it is not true. I just saw Claude at six o'clock yesterday evening. Everything was fine when I left him. Oh! My God, how can this tragedy be?"

As I cried, Paul comforted me by putting his arms around me and said,

"We all will go one day, now or later. Claude has gone and we must keep on going. We must be strong and positively face the future. Due to the political situation in Vietnam at the moment, my company decided for me to return to France sometime this month. I will write you and I want you to keep me informed about how you are doing, and if you are leaving Vietnam. I do not think this situation is going to get better. My other company friends are also getting their exit visas - - and returning home to France. You still can come to France if you want to. Please keep your spirit up because I have faith in you that you will do well wherever you are."

Paul gave me a comforting hug and said goodbye. Because of the death of Claude my destiny pointing to the United States instead of France became possible. The turning point of one's fate cannot be altered.

XXVI

National Traits

"Rain in Saigon - Rain in Hanoi," a popular song of Saigonees, used to play on the national radios in the city. The rain in Saigon was beautiful, a music of lovers, and a song of love. The rain in Hanoi was misty with a chilly wind, and bleak sky. Because the city of Saigon had modern architecture and wide boulevards and streets, it also had many tourist attractions.

The city in Hanoi had ancient imperial palaces, temples, and tombs. People from both cities were different in their modes of living and habits. These people did not get along well because of their differences. In 1954, when the refugees from Hanoi city came to Saigon for political asylum, it took those refugees a number of years to adjust to the way of life of Saigonees. One incident occurred when a Saigonee made a statement in regards to the business deals of his partner. He said, "I have looked into the market but can not find any sources." The guy from Hanoi city, would say, "Merchandise is hard to find in the market like hen's teeth."

Dialects and Mannerism were the two major problems and sometime caused friction between the two people. People from Hanoi city were very tight. Every penny was worth something when they spent it — must be worth it. These people had lived in Saigon city for a while and got used to the living standards of the majority so as to become compatible.

I was always puzzled about this. Hanoi city was where all the one time Kings of our country lived. But why were the people from Hanoi city so cheap in their way of living? Most of our famous histories were written about the victories of Hanoi people, but what I knew were the hordes of refugees with nothing but a pack on their backs as they arrived in Saigon city. I have never been in Hanoi. But I am sure that I would like to visit its cities at least one time in my life time to see the original city where our Kings rested.

During the war between North and South Vietnam, I had many friends who were song writers, musicians, and poets. Those people were the soldiers without guns, ammunitions and grenades. The war took many hearts and brains of our writers to write explosive songs, music, and poems which broke down the wall and fortress of the Vietnamese Communists (VC). They were patriots of the South and the only guns they had were their voices, pens, and musical instruments. One of the blockbuster songs was written by a friend of mine who was popular in the theaters, live shows, radios, and TV, in English:

"The entire people... Have you heard the nation is at war? Rancor for a long time. Should it be war or peace?"

Voices of people in the background....WAR!

I believed in heaven and hell, writers were very courageous and straight. They cannot write anything else but the truth, the facts of their knowledge of the current situation of people in the South. Since then all men from all ages registered to fight the war. They were the frontiers in our many battlefields. They died for the great cause of the South Vietnamese. They were the sacred examples for the Vietnamese youngsters in our later generation.

XXVII

Deadly Appointment

The young sergeant showed up at my door and politely handed me the yellow envelope (the color which military official's used for 'mail outs'). The sergeant went on,

"Ma'am, the general would like to see you at dinner time this Saturday evening. He is looking forward to seeing you. Thank you."

I visited the general and avoided driving my car. The reason was because of the possibility of future terrorist attacks — so the taxi was the best choice. I got in the taxi cab to make the appointment. In the taxi, two blocks away from the headquarters, I was thinking,

"Is this going to be the end, or the beginning of my destiny?"

I could turn around and forget the deadly appointment. Then, I thought,

"He is too big a man for him to find me anywhere in the country, unless I left for another country."

I must have had courage. I was on my way to face the general.

It was a big three-story building used as their headquarters. At a large conference table, dinner was displayed. I told myself,

"This looks like the last meal for the death row prisoners."

I felt like a caught a bad cold, my nerves were stiff, and my feet stuck to the floor. The general saw all that. He asked me to sit down and politely in his gesture showed me the chair at the other end of the table, and he said,

"Do not be afraid, my dear. You have nothing to be afraid of when you are in this building."

I gasped,

"But when I am out of this building, I will have a lot of worry, sir."

He presented me with,

"Here are my emergency phone numbers. All you have to do is call here. All the sergeants and corporals you saw here will take care of it."

The general raised his brandy glass to toast with me in the same distinct manner as he had since my first minutes at his office building.

"Please eat..." The general said.

In war time, all those lenient mannerism could lead to a peaceful death for anyone. The book of Confucianism and Lão Tû of China had taught that many of us would be deadly weapons which were the ones with the mind of gentleness. During the dinner the young sergeant kept filling up the glasses of brandy for us. Now, the general asked,

"Are you a reliable source for your friends in connecting with the Vietnamese National Liberation Front? Is that true? Please tell me."

I took a deep breath. At least I knew what to expect from the general. I told him,

"First, please release my younger brother. He had been taken away for three days by the local police. Second, my friends were the poor business folks. They bought what they can sell to make a buck for a living. They were the people of no discrimination. Their buyers were from all over the country."

Here, the general halted,

"You are definitely correct. But if this supply and demand continues to go on, we will have a deficit in our military budget and continuous interior corruptions of the armies. As you know military imports and exports were tax exempt. Business like that could bring our military armies to a deep ditch for your friends to dig."

I did not want to give up so easily. I said to the general,

"The economy in Vietnam depends on the buying power from the city of Saigon and the selling to worldwide. I mean other allies, whoever had money. Let us say there is an innocent man. But if you put one million dollars cash in front of him, he will change his mind.

"Sir, I would like to entertain you with a little folk story from a town in China. Winter in China was very long. Poor people in town did not have enough warm clothes or food for days. They had to dig on the ground and eat the black coal which retained the heat in their body to endure the severe cold of their winter. When summer came, those people died because of the coal they ate last winter. Life is so precious even though just to live for a short while longer. Can you blame the people?"

The general's face had a glow of satisfaction. He complimented,

"It is very interesting — you made your point. How about a toast for your victory? You convinced me that everyone has the right to live, very well done."

The general asked,

"Do you think it was right for the United States to drop bombs on North Vietnam?"

I replied,

"Firstly, the United States is fighting a war the same way it fought the war in Korea. Secondly, the United States tended to repeat their mistakes instead of trying something different. The United States was known for the use of heavy firepower. In another words, it would have been better to use non-violent tactics. You have got to win the people over before you win the war. Sometimes, the "pen is mightier than the sword."

"The United States fought the war in Korea and Japan but the United States can not fight Vietnamese style. They can not understand the way the Vietnamese Communists fight. The Vietnamese Communists know about their own birth rate. For instance, one hundred thousand Vietnamese babies would be born in a year, they knew that they can afford to loose fifty thousand to the war.

"When you come into somebody's house and stay there long enough, and know the inside information and if you were captured by the other side, then the people who want to overthrow the government must be told what you know. In such cases you have to make up some information in order to survive. You can not fight the war if you are divided. Because the Vietnamese know who is Vietnamese Communist and who is not. But you do not know this if you are divided from South Vietnamese. That is why you can not fight the war."

The general inquired,

"What do you think about the volunteers fighting the war in Vietnam?"

"They are very brave and courageous," I responded.

The general asked,

"How do you feel about the Buddhist monks protesting against the South Vietnamese government?"

I replied with caution,

"The Buddhist monks burned themselves to protest Catholicism. The government considered Catholicism as the national religion of the country. But actually Buddhism was there longer than Catholicism. The Vietnamese people are supposed to be a peace loving people. You can not just walk in and change their beliefs. If they are villagers and foreigners, you should talk about farming and how to raise livestock, and agriculture and make life tenable."

The four-star general of our allied army quoted,

"...only farmers and villagers were killed in the fighting. The intelligencia were protected."

I cut in quickly,

"General, are you questioning my intelligence? That is true; I am alive and sitting here with you. This subject could make an enormous debate. In my opinion, the farmers and the villagers have the right to live, too. To sort out the over-populated areas in the world by killing is not the best means of a solution. How about birth control pills for women and condoms for men including the directions of how to use them? I think it would work, sir."

The general remarked,

"April, you are a patriot, and a very considerate human being. Before I met you, I was hoping that you could shed light on the problems we are facing. And you did. Your friends are safe, and I want to thank you for your assistance. I bring this up in the coming conference of the year 2000 of the Buddhist religion of Vietnam."

* * * *

South Vietnam is a land of rich, natural resources. There is uranium, aluminum, zinc, oil and precious stones. This is not to mention, many gold mines.

Since South Vietnam was still developing agriculture and trade markets with the rest of the world, the United States Government offered South Vietnam twenty-five percent of all the natural resources found by expert engineers, geologists and machinery. With this aid, the excavations began. In the meanwhile, the U.S. Government also provided South Vietnam agricultural advisors aid in improving the growth of crops, greens and vegetables. It was a vast project throughout the South in the beginning. Workers began their work and managers were projecting daily the plan to have the job done. The farmers were joyous with their fruitful harvests.

People in the South started liking chewing gum because the French did not have chewing gum then, although the French had dropped lots of condoms from a small plane throughout the small towns. They did this so people would use them to control the population. I was a few years old at that time. I picked up one pack and opened it. I was frantically yelling, "Ha! Ha! BALLOON!"

In Saigon, "Spearmint Gum," was a Uniform Commercial Code for many of those working for the U.S. government. Those people recognized each other by giving out a piece of gum, even though they had not met one another before. When they saw the gum, they knew the other was their comrade. After many years the piece of chewing gum had became a connector for the friendship of Vietnamese and Americans in the South.

"What a mighty piece of gum!" I applaud.

"The Devils," advocated that South Vietnam was under the control of the American government because of modernization of the South in the Western style. The South was torn between

331

patriotism and a better life for all. Just look back at the war history. Who spent the most lives and money for the South? Americans! And those allies in action side by side with the Americans were there for many years in South Vietnam. Friends like that are few and far between. Americans that went to the South were well trained and educated to meet the Vietnamese standards and requirements in order to fit with common citizens in the South and the society of the elite. In those years, there were tremendous efforts to aid South Vietnam to bring it to a more modern lifestyle, without compromising Vietnamese culture. This was very challenging to the Americans while overseas and at home. Friendship is to give and share. Of course, Americans were given a share of the treasures of the South mostly because the South Vietnamese lacked techniques, money or the machinery to utilize their natural wealth. The American military were the police in the South to keep war turmoil down so the leaders of both countries could discuss and plan for further peace and new development for people in the South.

I and millions of Vietnamese all over the world are still expressing the great regret of the leaving of the Americans and the fall in Saigon, South Vietnam in 1975. The human rights agreement from President Jimmy Carter in 1976, allowed the Vietnamese refugee to go to America and start a new life on American soil. We all thank God for the opportunity to have our new beginning.

When I arrived in the United States, I got down on my knees, thanked God, and kissed the ground.

Confucius said: "Good harvest comes to those who work hard." The Vietnamese people absorbed the many teachings from the East, using it in their everyday lives with others.

The destiny of South Vietnam was only one day different. The Americans left one day too early; The North Vietnam was already sewing their white flags to surrender to the South. The South was given to the Northern leadership.

Meeting the allied general was an immense experience. This reminds me of a story of a Russian Queen.

Many years ago, there was a Queen who lived a celebrate life in the palace. Next to the Queen was a four-star General who carried out orders from the Queen. The general secretly fell in love with the Queen.

One day the palace held a ballroom dance for all the dignitaries in the government. The Queen had eyes for a young private who was the guard in the palace that evening. Thereafter, the Queen ordered the private to the palace to have dinner with her. The Queen revealed to the private her intention to marry him. The private was trembling as he explained to the Queen that he had a fiancée. The Queen felt insulted by the refusing of the private. The Queen decreed the private to die. He was imprisoned immediately.

The general now understood what the Queen was going through when she was rejected by the private. In the palace, the General consoled the Queen to feel at ease because there are other ways to solve this matter and still regain the honor of a Queen. The Queen agreed with the General to help her loving private and his fiancée go to a new world.

The passports were made up and new identities were made for the private and his fiancée with money to be happy ever after in the other world.

A scarecrow of the private was shot early the next morning. Thus, the Queen had shown the love she had for her man.

In this case there is life after death for the man whom the Queen adoringly loved.

XXVIII

Save Life Your Life Will Be Saved

My younger brother Long walked in and introduced me to his friend, Tim Cathai. Tim was a lieutenant in the Political-Warfare of the National Defense of the South Vietnamese government. Tim was tall, slim and had a rugged look. My younger brother seated Tim in the living room and then went to the refrigerator to get three cold drinks for us. Tim was very polite and well mannered. He was a graduate of the South Vietnamese Military Academy and was appointed as a military officer three years earlier, but he was leaving his job with the South Vietnamese Government. He did this because he was disappointed with the amount of government corruption. His past included rather important gang activities which involved him in extortion and acquiring and providing illegal weapons for gang members and other gang-related functions including armed robberies. Most of his victims were rather high level managers and operators of Saigon nightclub establishments. My younger brother was acquainted with him from previous days and he was not involved in any of those criminal activities.

The sale of illegal weapons in South Vietnam was very carefully watched and controlled by the corrupt authorities. They were of course deeply involved with the VC. Many of those individuals involved in gang type activities were also members from all levels of the military. These organized criminals operated in an exact same manner as the MAFIA in the West and only those that got in their way had anything to fear. However, innocent people would be wounded or killed accidentally in the cross fire.

One time, I dropped by the Grand Hotel Nightclub in Saigon. As usual, we meet with these managers to exchange ideas as to improve our businesses in order to attract tourists from the airport to our establishments. Room reservations, entertainment and food were our specialty. During one of the visits, a tall man in a formal dress approached me and asked me if I would join him. At his table there were six men. The tall man introduced his friends to me which gave me something to think about.

I asked myself, "What do they want from me?"

They were the men who made the collections for business protection. I told the tall man that I have no problem with anyone. The tall man told me if I do, he would protect me. He liked me because I was so cool. When I was at the tall man's table I was ready to face the worst. I felt I was at their mercy. Fortunately, they let me go and I safely went to the parking lot without being involved with them. Till this day, I can not understand why they let me go unharmed. Later I was told by one of the gang men that I was so cute, that he let me go and saved me there for his future bride.

Tim remarked to my younger brother and said,

"I wish to change my life style and go straight partly because of the failing health of my mother whom I adored greatly."

He was her only child.

My younger brother turned to me and implored,

"Tim needs our help, he needs a new start and we may be able to help him in that way. Can you, please?"

I remember when the Vietnamese Communists infiltrated throughout Saigon. Because of this, the curfew was strictly enforced around the clock to better apprehend those individuals. This strict enforcement lasted for a two-week period. This occurred on New Year's Eve of 1968. My younger brother, our mother, housekeeper, and I were the ones inside our home. In my younger brother's hand was a bayonet in case a VC were to break into the house at any moment. Also, he was worried of the unpredictable actions of the VC terrorists and what they might do. He was especially concerned because I was an owner of a large nightclub and dinner club, which involved me with many high level connections, not to mention my uncle who was Chief of Police of the whole Saigon of six million people.

The infiltration of the VC on New Year's Eve of 1968 was based on the secret agreement with Dr. Kissinger (The U.S.

Secretary of State). The VC had forty-eight hours to take over Saigon, which they were unable to accomplish. The military of South Vietnam were very forceful and informed the civilians about the impending danger. Thus, there were a significant number of people who were killed or wounded. These comprised of the military, civilians, and allies population.

"If Tim is sincere about changing his career, I will do anything within my power to help." I replied.

Tim had saved my brother's life on the other side of the city from a local gang, It was there that my younger brother was dating a high school girl. She lived in the territory of the local gang where he was visiting. They surrounded him, about fifteen of them with knives, batons, and oak stick. They were all in their twenties or younger and their faces showed their anger towards my younger brother. An older boy in the gang, medium in height and slim, instructed the others to get my younger brother down to his knees. The older gang leader exclaimed,

"Get him down; he is horning in on our territory"

The gang encircled my younger brother and snarled,

"To keep coming back here, you must have lots of guts."

My younger brother was not bothered with what the gang said. He used all his concentration on the gang's imminent sudden attack. He lowered his body a couple inches at his knees and his arms he put in a fighting position. He was ready to bring some of the gang down with him, if necessary. At that moment, fear was neither in his mind nor survival; but death was at hand. He knew he was going to die taking a couple members with him. Because of the fear within the gang that my younger brother instilled in them, they momentarily hesitated making their attack. The gang was large in size but small in courage. Due to his courageous stand he was able to ward off their unwarranted attack.

My brother's determined look of power and willingness to fight to the bitter end was what saved him. My younger brother was alone. Tim was in a cafe next door and saw a young man fighting against the gang by himself. Tim came out with his gun and shot a couple rounds in the air, which panicked them, the gang members scattered in all directions. That was how my younger brother and Tim became close friends.

I reassured them that I could help,

"Tim can stay in my home until such a time his situation would be worked out and he can work in my nightclub as a waiter."

While Tim was staying at my home, we always were mutually respectful. In Tim's eyes, I was a shining star from the sky. and fortunately. I was able to help him with a new beginning at my young age of twenty-two. Tim was twenty-seven, quiet, obstinate and daring. I helped him to make a good change in his life style. Tim substantially followed my suggestions in furthering his career. He was a good looking man, rugged, sturdy and had a luminous bronze complexion.

I told myself,

"Any man with his looks is awesome."

Tim and I kept close but distant so I could pursue my business goals. Because I was so ambitious in business I put my social life on the back burner.

One day I was not feeling well and had to stay in bed and Tim went to the kitchen and made me a cup of hot tea. He said to my housekeeper,

"I will make the tea and bring it to her in bed."

Knock, Knock!

"Come on in." I said.

Tim gently lowered the cup of tea to my bed and said politely,

"I hope this cup of tea will make you feel better."

I thanked him and complimented with,

"You are so thoughtful and I feel better already. I have got to get out of bed because the dinner club and the bicycle business need me there.

Tim suggested,

"Your health is very important and you should stay in bed for a couple days."

I replied,

"If I slow down, I feel that I am falling behind on my business matters. I want to be very successful at forty so I can relax and enjoy my life. What do you think?"

Tim answered,

"You are absolutely correct. You have set your goal and you are slowly but steadily getting there. I only hope to be a little part in your life to help you, your business interests and anything else because your wish is my command."

Tim's words moved me and I was a little distracted from what he said. I kept my feelings to myself and tried not to show it to Tim. I responded,

"You are educated and a good-looking man. You will be a wheeler dealer one day. Right now you need some patience to get over the rough period in your life. Everybody needs someone sometime.

Tim declared,

"Thanks for your comfort and confidence in me. I will retire to the living room so you can rest for the night. Please let me know if there is anything that you want me to do."

Tim left my bedroom. I then laid my head down on the pillow. I felt better after I drank the tea and the caffeine in the tea somehow cleared up my mind. I thought of the success of my business in the coming years. The thoughts of how nice looking Tim was there as well but I pushed them out of my mind.

A month went by and Tim had been working every day at my dinner club. He chose not to have days off so he could save up some money to get out on his own. His mother lived by herself in another town approximately a hundred and thirty kilometers from Saigon. She was suffering with a heart problem but was unable to go to a hospital because the cost of medical care was so expensive; also Vietnam had no social security, Medicaid nor health insurance. Most Vietnamese people paid their own medical expenses. At dinner, my younger brother, Long, told me,

"Sister, Tim's mother had a stroke and is hospitalized at Bình Dủỏng Hospital. The hospital refused to further treatment until they paid the bills upfront."

I instructed Tim,

"Tim, you take off from work for a few days to see your mother. I will bring you some money from the bank tomorrow and you can pay me back later. I hope it is not too late to save her life. You should have told me earlier."

Tim explained,

"After you have done everything for me I can not bother you with more problems. I was going to ask you if I could leave town tomorrow to see my mother."

"Is this an emergency? Do not ever hesitate to tell me something like that next time. I will advance you one hundred thousand dồng (equivalent one thousand dollars) to pay the hospital and let me know about the rest of the bills when you get back here." I explained.

Tim left Saigon at noon for Bình Dủởng province. With the money I gave Tim, his mother was able to receive decent medical treatment at the hospital and recovered from her ill health a week later. The day I left Saigon for the United States, Tim told me,

"How can I ever repay you?"

"You already have! You are on your own and your mother has her good health and the two of you need each other. Just be good and do not get in trouble because those days of your thunder are gone. You are a different man now." I said.

Tim sadly said,

"I will miss you!"

I responded,

"I will miss you, too. Give my love to your mother and I wish you all the best of luck. I know you feel that I have given you a lot but have you ever thought that without you that day my younger brother would have lost his life. So I helped you and your mother partly to repay you. Our family tradition states, that if you do business with us honestly, you will always earn extra profits. So, we have helped one another."

Tim was tough and smart. He understood my philosophical ideas.

He stood solemnly on the outside patio where the summer flower vines were attached to the wall and over head rafters. The sun reflected on Tim's face and perspiration was visible. Those were the last good minutes with Tim before I left for the airport and I boarded the plane to the United States.

XXIX

Turbulence in Little Saigon

Saigon is the jewel of Southeast Asia, an international exchange market, a major business stopping off point of businessmen from all over the world.

Time moved quickly and Christmas was around the corner. The markets were busy; shops and restaurants were full of people were coming and going. Christmas in Saigon had become a yearly tradition, especially for oriental Christian believers and other interested parties. Christmas is the season which brings joy and the exchanging of gifts between family members and friends.

It was after ten o'clock on Christmas Eve. I left my two partners in charge of our restaurant to go attend a dance contest with André and our friends at Maxim, the number one nightclub of Saigon.

André had invested twenty thousand U.S. Dollars in my seafood and kapok export business to France, Italy and Belgium. He was one of several investors in my seafood and kapok business. The truth was, as a staff member of the DAO, delegated by the United States Government, André could not be involved in private enterprise. However, André was not the only one who broke this rule. Beside his investment with my seafood and kapok business, André was engaged in the black market. He and his associates met every Tuesday at his home and on Thursdays met at one of the other's home where they had a poker party. André had three close friends who also worked for the United States Government, one with the Central Intelligence Agency (CIA), one with the Central Investigation Department (CID), and one with the DAO. They all had business involvement with André, except the one with the CIA, whom was Nathan.

Three months prior to the South Vietnamese government's order for all the foreigners to leave, all business contracts or connections inside or outside the country were cancelled, whether small or large in nature. Because of this, my seafood and kapok business were cancelled. According to my agreement with André, he lost his money including principle and interest. One time I stopped by to see a married couple, a security Captain with Mission Warden Office, who was married to a Vietnamese woman. She let me know that our mutual friend, André, had consulted with her and stated his great sadness of the loss of his money with my business and held me responsible. When I heard that, I was very disappointed because I had a business engagement with a person with no backbone. Furthermore, André had lost all other business engagements in the black market, not only with my business but everything else he was involved in. It was out of my hands. I had no control of this and he was stupid to think it was my fault. Besides, he ignored all the profits he had pocketed.

I left my restaurant about five in the evening to go to Maxim, where André and our friends were waiting for all us to join together to celebrate the festivities. That night, after I left my restaurant, gun shots occurred in front of my restaurant. The police identified a gang leader well known in the city, which the authorities had been looking for. At the time of this shooting in front of my dinner club, my female singer accidentally caught a bullet to her head while she was getting out of a taxi and was instantly killed. While running, the fleeing man ran in a zigzag manner, which made him a difficult target. Unfortunately, the singer stepped out of the taxi at that particular moment, when the bullets were for the fleeing man. The singer was arriving to perform at my nightclub that night. When he came in along with other gang members, Tim Cathai recognized them and immediately called the police. In a few minutes, the police arrived and that was the reason the shooting took place. This was Tim's manner in expressing his appreciation for my help to him. During those times of disastrous situations in my lifetime, I always felt there was a supernatural power watching over me to insure my survival.

Another occurrence, at a nearby well-known establishment catering to fine clientele, I planned on dropping in on the owner to present a business proposition. A group of Japanese businessmen representing Akai, Teac, Sharp, Sanyo and Mitsubishi arrived an hour later at my restaurant. Their late arrival was due to a weather delay of their airplane at the Tokyo airport. Because of this late arrival it saved my life. During that time while I was waiting for the Japanese businessmen at my restaurant, there was a ferocious dynamite explosion at the Caruso restaurant, which resulted in more than twenty dead (customers and workers). I could have been one of the corpses laid out or one of the forty-seven people seriously injured from the blast. That was my lucky fortune again. The supreme being was guarding me again. How lucky can one person be? This was the state of condition in Vietnam at that time. These occurrences took place any time, any place, anywhere, especially at public places. All public places including the Caruso nightclub had excellent security but because of fear of scaring off customers, they kept most of security behind the scene. In another words, they did not want to make the nightclub look like a war zone.

I escaped the man with the white sheet and sickle again, but the danger never ended. Shortly after that I had an appointment at the Air France ticketing office to make a reservation to travel to Tokyo in the spring of 1969. Just before I arrived, a rocket from the VC hit sanitation workers with their truck. As I got there, I saw torn bodies everywhere. During that time in Vietnam there was so much violence by the VC, a person's survival was totally a matter of luck, and I always felt that luck was in my favor. Being ten minutes early or late at the wrong time could easily cost one's life. Because of the fear in people's minds back then in Vietnam, people regularly were late thinking this would increase their chances of surviving.

Vietnamese people are innately peace loving and family oriented. Also, they are very industrious and business-minded for many centuries. The reason cruelties occur during war is because war is hell. The dark side of all comes out and unfortunately tragedies often happen.

XXX

Maximum Exposure

I registered to vote for the election of the President of South Vietnam, which was my first time to vote. The candidate, whom I had voted for, was from Huế, the central part of Vietnam. He spoke with a southern accent, which impressed me highly. Since he acquired an understanding of the southerner's point of view, he was immediately popular.

Mr. Thiệu was successful in becoming President of South Vietnam. South Vietnam had become a Democracy and was called the Republic of Vietnam. South Vietnam felt a happiness that never existed before and everyone worked together with a co-operative spirit. Business managers worked at their desks, mechanics worked with their tools in their garages and farmers worked in their fields, etc. There were no sales taxes but other taxes such as income tax, property tax and import and export taxes, and these applied to every citizen throughout the country of South Vietnam.

When the President's term of re-election took place and the country changed into a fully Democratic society, this big change in the government's system caused a great deal of confusion in everyone's lives. Everybody wanted equality and freedom with equal rights. The farmers wanted to become active in the politics of the country with the new Democracy. The mechanics, likewise, wanted to take an active part in the political arena. If a farmer wanted to be a senator, even without a single day spent in school, how could he possibly reach that height without the necessary education? Many of the tens of thousands in the country were ill prepared to take on the responsibility of their new freedom. They needed to be able to be an adequate watch dog to see that the newly elected bureaucrats were not working for their own financial gain instead of the good of the country. Thus, the amount of corruption mushroomed.

An incident occurred during New Year's Eve called the Tết Offensive of 1968. Thousands of people in the city were suddenly made homeless because of the attacks from the VC against the South Vietnamese Armies and several thousand homes were destroyed during the onslaught. US Secretary of Defense McNamara had submitted a proposal to the United States Government for financial aid to those people who had lost their home and who were the victims of those attacks.

The United States Government granted twenty-five thousand U.S. Dollars to each victim of the Tết Offensive in 1968, which lost their home. The Tidal Waves newspaper was shut down permanently because the publication it made concerning the grabbing of the money for the housing compensation. Those people that worked for the newspaper were suddenly out of work. The government of Mr. Thiệu's regime gave the homeless people ten aluminum sheets and two bags of cement, and Mr. Thiệu and his compatriots got all the money. Mr. Thiệu and his associates pocketed the twenty-five thousand dollars of each homeless person. This created a feeling of distrust amongst the people of the South. Once this happened, it was the end of his regime.

Mr. Thiệu's governmental corruption was enormous and easily seen. After six years in power he left the country in disgrace. He was very corrupted and lacked the will-power to stay honest and to overcome the many difficulties of the newly formed Democratic Southern Society.

During a fit of rage, one of the President's four-star general shot at him but missed killing him. The general was so much angered at the thought of him stealing the money from the people who lost their homes and who were supposed to receive each twenty-five thousand dollars from the United States for the loss of their homes. This is just one small isolated case of an example in the Thiệu's government.

XXXI

Enchanted Love

"Why you are so late?" Lucile asked.

Lucile went on,

"You have to pay for coming here so late, Jack."

Jack replied,

"Do not talk about penalty! It is coming out my asshole. Government authorities have me by the nut."

Lucile was from Manila city in the Philippines. She got into the United States for the same reason as others from the Indochina war. She was working in the Mess Hall of the American Army in her home town where she met Jack. Jack was twenty-two and a Private-First-Class (PFC) in the army. Jack was a cook and had to peel potatoes everyday. Lucile was hired to help Jack peel potatoes, one at a time. Each potato skin filled up barrel after barrel. Everyday when Lucile got home, her mother inquired what Lucile had learned in the American kitchen. With joy Lucile told her mother that the PFC boss in the kitchen taught her how to peel potatoes in an awkward position. Lucile's mother was very enthusiastic and she cried with joy,

"Keep up with it, Lucile. Someday you can make yourself a PFC "boss" in the American kitchen. I am sure that opportunity will come in no time. Remember to tell your boss that I am counting on him, everyday."

Time slipped by, Lucile met Jack in the United States. They talked so much of the wonderful times working in the Mess Hall of the American Army in the Philippines. Now Jack is working for a major hotel at May Berry in Atlanta. Friends called him the "Chief Engineer." On the day when the floor of the kitchen was wet, he tripped with all the dishes flying to the floor, like flying saucers shown on the American Television shows.

However, Jack and Lucile had their betrothal, a formal tradition in the Far East which they maintained. Lucile was working in a textile factory. This time Lucile was learning something new, her modern machine that she worked on everyday. Back home Lucile would have to use her hands all day long. The job was hard and the noise of the factory even made it harder to endure.

Lucile was my roommate, when she first arrived from the Philippines she found my ad in the newspaper and we became friends since then. It was a coincidence when Jack was renting a room in a building of a friend of mine. Jack had been talking about his good time in Manila with my friend. Jack always praised Lucile as a wonderful oriental woman. She was luscious, lots of femininity and most of all she was submissive to Jack, and she was lots of fun to be with. Jack told Ben, his landlord,

"I know a girl in the Philippines named Lucile. I wonder if she is somewhere in the United States. We worked together in the Mess Hall of the American Army in the Philippines.

Ben replied,

"I know a girl name Lucile who is sharing an apartment with a friend of mine from South Vietnam. Maybe this is the Lucile you have been talking about. If you wish Jack, I could bring you to meet April so you can find out if Lucile who is living with April is your old friend."

Jack was so enthusiastic and said,

"Please take me to meet them."

Ben and I arranged a dinner at my place and invited Jack to come over. Here, Jack met Lucile. He thought he would never see her again. Their dreams came true. They were getting married and have a family of their own.

XXXII

Friend / Shadow of Greed

Dan's voice on the telephone echoed in my ears,

"Is this Voice of America (VOA) headquarters?"

Dan was a humorous fellow. We had been friends for a few years. He was Colonel in the United States Navy Press in Saigon when he was thirty-five. Dan had risked his life to save some of his friends, the doctors and attorneys working for the United States Aid (USAID), one of the biggest military organizations of the United States in Southeast Asia. Dan drove through Saigon during curfew hours to bring his friends to the plane waiting at the Saigon airport. His bravery and courageous attitude was remarkable. With elation, I yelled in the telephone,

"Hi Dan, where in the world are you? Tell me how do you know where I am?"

363

Dan replied,

"I got your phone numbers from André in Oklahoma city. Was he a sneaky guy...? Did you get back the money you spent on the two people you had brought back to United States?"

"No, I did not, after we came to the United States, their sister and brother-in-law canceled the deal they made with me. I considered it was a loss because I had no proof of it. The only proof I had was André. But André was loaded up with money from a Saigon-To States-Deal with the President's family of Shell Corporation of South Vietnam."

Dan asked,

"So, what are you going to do about that?"

I replied,

"Nothing! If you hear anything, please let me know. I might go up there sometime for old time's sake this year and will look you up."

On the line Dan's voice with force and assurance,

"Keep up with your writings. Everybody knows you are writing a good book and I would like to be the first one to read it. I am now working for a news department at the Pentagon in Washington D.C. I know many writers and journalists who give you moral support from us. I am getting divorced in the next few months. Please take my phone numbers and call me when you need me, or for any reasons."

* * * *

Prior to leaving Saigon for the United States my younger brother dashed into my office to see me in an emergency. He asked,

"Sister, could I see you alone?"

In the office alone with him, He told me that things will be different in the city in three months. Everybody will want to be a VC, and he wanted my opinion. He said,

"Please hurry, Sister. I have to go now."

After a few moments of deep thought, I told him,

"The VC waves will be all over the city of Saigon, whether you want it or not you will have to become a VC Our American allies had an old saying:

"If you cannot beat them, then join them," in Vietnamese."

My younger brother was in the military Post Exchange (PX) and Commissary Food Supply business. I have learned afterward that all his military friends were able to survive with all VCs in Saigon city. In our bible, the Buddhist philosophies taught many of us that if you save lives, your life will be saved.

Obviously, American philosophies had saved some lives — in Vietnam. My younger brother is now married and has two beautiful little girls and his friends who were former military men are now surviving with much gratitude to the Americans. I got their letters; they said they would love to see the United States of America.

XXXIII

Ultimate Hour

Heather, my grandmother, lifted Linh's head upon her lap and nurtured Linh with her mixed herb medicines. My grandmother was an oriental doctor in their own town and a close neighbor. Linh was a mother of two little children, a girl seven and a boy five. Linh's husband was one of the Việt-Minh (Vietnamese Unanimous) leaders during the French domination. He has not been home for number of months due to his job and responsibilities in Việt-Minh. His wife Linh fell ill since his last visit, several months ago. Between Heather, the doctor, and her daughter, Shana was twenty-three, married and had two sons, one three and one two. Shana and her husband were separating so Shana and her two sons came home and lived with her mother. While helping her mother, Shana also traveled from afar as a merchant to make a living for her and her two sons.

The funeral for Linh took place. My grandmother, the doctor, let her rest in peace in the fifteen acres of land which my grandmother owned, and took care of the two little children until their father came home.

During that time, Shana had to travel out of town. This time she had to cross a jungle to get the merchandise. She was buying food products and fabrics from Cambodia. She was a saleswoman and a firm believer of her faith, the Cao Đài religion. Her cargo was enroute, when fifteen men in black uniforms stopped it.

"Your identification please." The black uniformed soldier demanded,

Shana showed him her religion ID. The soldier in the black uniform seemed like the chief of the group. He ordered her to be taken to the fortress. There she was held for five days before someone came to her rescue. The interrogation began:

The question: "Why have you traveled in a forbidden area?"

"I did not know this was a forbidden area, until you stopped me." Shana replied.

"Your status is very suspicious. You are a firm believer of the Cao Đài religion which has been dealing with French connections."

"Religion is a place for all the public, such as French, Hungarian, or Mongolian who could worship the same faith. I have not any connections with government or politics. I believe in God and there is only one God for all mankind."

The papers of Shana's persecution came to Duston, Chief Commander of the Việt-Minh, the father of the two little children whom Shana's mother was taking care of. Duston rode on a horse for three nights in the woods, to arrive on time to save Shana. As the horse and Duston arrived, the soldiers stated in the fortress:

"Salute! Commander Duston."

"Captain, this fortress is under your command. I want to know who ordered the arrest of my wife Shana." Duston stated. He continued on:

"My wife came a long way to see me and this is how your men are treating her? Captain, I decrease your rank to Sergeant. And, if she looses any of her sight from the result of your treatment you will be decreased to private. Do you understand captain?"

"Yes sir, I am sorry for the misunderstanding. I promise you that I will take more caution next time." The captain pleaded.

"Captain, there is no more next time. You almost executed my wife, if I had not arrived in time to stop you from killing my wife. What if you did, how could you repay me? Now, leave me alone with my wife."

The captain said, "Yes, sir... - at once."

"Thank you, Duston, you saved my life!" Shana remarked.

Duston said,

"You are my wife that is all you have got to know. I will escort you out of this place and send you home. You and your mother had saved my wife and the kids. But now is not the time to talk about that. I want to help you just as much as your family has helped mine. Please give me this chance to repay you. I am a big man but could not fulfill my responsibilities with my family: My wife died in your arms, and I could not come home to her funeral."

In this way, the Chief Commander of Việt-Minh was able to repay my grandmother and mother for the help his family received. And the relationship had been fulfilled. Just as the Buddhist teaching states: "You save a life, and then your life will be saved."

* * * *

Harrison, twenty-five, was a son of a wealthy landlord in the West side of South Vietnam, where the best rice harvest in the whole country comes from. Farmers in this area usually worked three months out of a year when they planted rice. The rest of the year they were doing something else until the harvest arrived. The monsoon came during the months of January through March, and that was the rice planting season in the West. Farmers were well off and lived in a fine style in the whole of South Vietnam. Rice was the largest crop in the West and was exported to Malaysia, the Philippines, Laos, Cambodia, Hong Kong, Singapore and other neighboring countries of Vietnam.

Harrison could not relax that night. The prophecy of a fortune-teller was still bothering him. So, he left his wife and his six month old baby girl home before the disastrous prophecy might happen to his family. He must desert them for their own sake.

Fortune-tellers in the East play a very important role. They have psychic powers to tell the people about future events. Their prophecy could become most valuable. Harrison was told to leave his home town.

At midnight, Harrison kissed his child and wife who were asleep. Harrison left home without saying goodbye. In the morning when his family woke, they did not know when he left home until twenty-two years later. His ex-wife explained to Harrison that if he had not left that night, the VC were already looking for him. He was good at music, and he knew seven musical instruments. In town, people followed him everywhere he performed his music. This made him become popular with the VC. Either he joined them or beat them, or, his last solution was to leave home that night. That night he was born again.

Harrison's music continued successfully and the government of Vietnam began to admire Harrison, who had only his music to win the hearts of people throughout the country. The French were part of the government system there. They felt that Victor Hugo and Alexander Rose came from France and invented the Vietnamese language. Therefore, Vietnam was part of France's territory and the French were the administrators of Vietnam for a hundred years.

The colonel, the Chief of National Administration greeted Harrison at the office headquarters, and said,

"Please be seated, Harrison." The colonel handed out a box of 555 cigarettes and asked Harrison to help himself.

Harrison said carefully: "Thank you, Colonel, but I do not smoke."

"How about having a glass of champagne with me?"

Harrison was smart enough to know that he must be reasonable in certain instances. He should not say no at all times, especially at a time like this. Harrison politely accepted the offer from the Colonel.

The arrangement between military personnel was made. Harrison was appointed a First Lieutenant in the administration. He was the officer in charge of military personnel rosters and recruits of the army. The government authorities were smart. They gave Harrison a job that suited his will, a job that was nonviolent with a sense of responsibility. He could not kill a chicken so put him in a clean job to make him believe that he does not have to kill to survive. So let someone else do the dirty job for him.

Harrison knew all about this. But what can a man do who is between the devil and deep blue sea? If the government did not get him, the VC would. Harrison married my mother, and I was born.

People throughout the West loved Harrison's music. His music had brought them to reality of the fact they were under French control. They supported him. One day Harrison received his military assignment to go out of town one hundred miles with the troops. People supported him from the VC side, too. His search and attack missions were successful and not a single man got killed, or hurt. As a result, Harrison was promoted to Major.

My mother wanted to be helpful to our family. She ran a lumber yard and men worked in the woods. Business was going very well. It helped our family budget and made less pressure on my father. A business competitor of ours used their black mail by dropping a message connected with the VC in the woods. Because our business was traveling in the deep woods to buy lumber, the French were in power in the government. They were fearful of my father's actions thinking that my father was connected with the Vietnamese Revolution, and the VC against them. With alibi in hand, the French put my father in detention the same day they got the message. There was no trial or grand jury. My father received the judgment from a one star general of the army — "Death sentence." It was a barbaric action of French military justice in Vietnam.

At four o'clock in the morning, the fourteen prisoners were executed by the firing squad, supposedly including my father. But a prisoner on death row had gone in my fathers place so he could escape death. He said,

"I committed murder and I am going to die anyhow. I go for you in the morning. The French do not identify the prisoners like us. They just want fourteen men to die from this prison. I hope you can do something in your power to alleviate the penalty of the prisoners, later."

Years later, the French withdrew from Vietnam. Our country was then independent. My father was appointed the Chief of Army Instruction. He was going to churches and temples and convinced them to write petitions to our government for amnesties for the prisoners once a year on Christ's birthday, and Buddhist Anniversary of the 2000 year. The petition passed the Congress and was granted by our President. Every year the prisoners throughout the country were receiving the same blessing. Their imprisonment could be cut back once a year.

My father's promise was finally kept. Perhaps the prisoner who died years ago for my father must be very pleased about the achievement of my father.

XXXIV

Love Never Ending in Japan

Haruhiko and Nishikawa walked in the office and looked around for the director of our office. I greeted both in Japanese,

"Konichi Anata-wa Nan desuka?"

In English it means "Good afternoon, what can I do for you sirs?"

I showed the two young Japanese gentlemen to our director's office. Ten minutes later, Haruhiko and Nishikawa came to see me at my desk and requested an extension of their visas. I was in charge of visa extension for the International Air Travel in Saigon. I was nineteen, Haruhiko twenty-two, and Nishikawa was twenty-three. Both were students of Tokyo University of International Economy. They traveled to Malaysia, Singapore, the Philippines and South Vietnam for their studies. Haruhiko looked like an oriental duke with a whitish baby face and was seemingly very shy. His heart was growing for me, the young lady who was working on the extension of his visa. It was not an easy job for me, because their visas were already expired and they must be on the plane leaving Saigon in twenty-four hours. Nishikawa was a little more aggressive. He did most of all the talking. I found out that Haruhiko fell in love with me when I came to Tokyo in the early spring of 1969.

A year later, I went to Tokyo for a cultural research study. I met Haruhiko and Nishikawa. They had graduated from school. Haruhiko was the bank manager and Nishikawa was a businessman. The three of us went all over town to restaurants, shops, and the theater to see Spring Dance of the Japanese. When evening came, Nishikawa shook hands with me to withdraw to his study at home and leave Haruhiko with me. He then said,

"Haruhiko has been waiting all this time for this moment to be alone with you, April. I will see you tomorrow if you have the time."

I told Nishikawa,

"The news reporter of Fuji Television in Tokyo, who was a friend of mine, wanted to have lunch with me tomorrow. So maybe I will see you with Haruhiko the day after tomorrow."

At my Daiichi hotel, alone with Haruhiko in the cocktail lounge, I was sitting across the table. His legs crossed over mine. With determination, Haruhiko said,

"I love South Vietnamese people, even though I was not there long enough to fight the communists by your side. I have been praying to God that I can see you again, and God did grant my wishes for you are here now."

He kept on,

"Across the ocean God had brought you safely to the land of Japan. I would like to feel your hand, to feel you, that you are real... -

I responded,

"I am here, and I am real. Can you feel my hand? My blood stream is flowing in my body system. Japan is a very beautiful country and a most powerful economic nation in the whole wide world. But I must return home with my family, and friends. They need me there. I am an unarmed soldier, and a prayer without a church. If I have the power, I would like to build a free hospital, larger church or temple for people who have misfortunes."

Haruhiko could not stand away from me many inches; he reached over the cocktail table and kissed my lips, following with these words,

"My sweetheart, you must become a President of South Vietnam, you talk like a president, and you think like a president."

I replied,

"Thank you, I only hope there is no more killing in my country so I can come and go as I please to Japan to see you, Haruhiko.

I continued on,

"It is hard to be a president; he can not go out or do things alone. He seldom has a private moment. His every moment is constantly scrutinized. His statements are carefully analyzed. A private citizen has ample freedom and privacy — far more than a President. A President carries enormous responsibilities and duties to his country and his people. If I were to be a President, my goals would be to encourage everyone to relax more rather than always being involved with serious business. I was born with the idea of having freedom in thought and spirit. Rather than being tied up with too much work and no time to enjoy life. You can kill a person but not his idea. My idea is to have as much freedom as possible. Since the President is working for the people, I hope he can do some good for his people."

Haruhiko listened to my explanation of why I did not want to be a President. He sat upright in the lounge chair tense with emotion.

To clear up the tense conversation between us, I sang a lovely Japanese song to Haruhiko,

"Anataga Kanda, Koyubi ga itai

Kino no yoru-no, Koyubi ga itai.

Sotto kuchibiru oshiatete, anata-no koto shinonde miruno."

In English this means:

"The little finger you bit, hurts.

Last night's little finger hurts.

I miss you as I touch my lips on the little finger."

Haruhiko could not wait any longer and reached over the cocktail table in the hotel lounge and with both of his warm hands, lifted my face up and kissed me passionately on the lips.

I went on,

"I say these things to you, not because I want to win you over. But because in the war, people from North and South are not allowed to listen or hear from each other's point of view. At times, one could be in serious trouble with the government only because he heard things from the other side. Therefore, during those days when one exchanged views with others they keep it confidential.

By the way, your name sounds like a girl's name. How did your parents pick that name for you?"

Haruhiko explained,

"Haru is the Spring. Hiko is a person. So Haruhiko is Mr. Spring, don't you like my name?

I refrained,

"So you are the Spring, a season of cherry blossoms, and a season of birds singing in trees. It is very good, I like it."

"Do not kid yourself and do not fall apart for a war-torn country folk! This is because our better future is far away." I teased Haruhiko.

Haruhiko was persistent,

"The war-torn country made the folks special, well-trained individuals and brave. I always loved and admired those qualities of the Vietnamese. And, you are one good example. You are young and have lots of courage; you did not turn your back on your country to forget all about the many problems. That is why I am here, to support, and to love you."

Haruhiko overwhelmed me. His explanation had a lot to do with his studies about the war in Vietnam. He was not despondent when I tried to get him to give up on me. His feeling for me was as strong as his feeling about the war. We were the good neighbors, friends, allies etc...

I inserted the key into the lock to open the door. Haruhiko stepped aside so I could walk in my hotel room before him. I looked for the switch. As my hand reached it, I felt his hand on my hand pushing away from the light switch. He lifted me up in his arms and carefully set me down on the bed. The night was long and easy. He was so nice, so wonderful.

Haruhiko lived three hundred miles from my hotel in Tokyo. He drove many hours earlier to Tokyo to see me. His parents owned a drug store. It was a two-story building with their home on the second floor. His parents greeted me with a smile. In Japanese, they asked me to come in the tea room upstairs. Haruhiko guided me to the room. Japanese are very meticulous in every aspect. There was a flower arrangement on a square table in the middle of the room and four pillows on the floor,

Japanese style. He indicated for me to sit on one of the pillows lying on the floor. He then kissed my lips and said,

"I will have Miko, my younger sister, keep you company. I have a few things at the bank to take care of. I will be back and see you at lunch. Please enjoy your visit at our home."

A few minutes after he left, Miko walked in with a tray of food in her hand. She sat the tray down on her lap while resting her knees on the pillow. She said in Japanese,

"Dozo, oishi desu."

It means in English: "Please eat, it is delicious."

While distributing the dishes on the table for me, Miko was very friendly and nice to be around. Miko asked me,

"Do you like Japan?"

She continued on,

"My brother spoke very highly of you before you arrived in Japan."

I said,

"Your brother was right. I was the talk of the town in my country.

Here I paused, and said,

"I am just kidding, Miko. Something about your brother made him a very special person to me. He is young and energetic with a lot of courage, too."

Miko stated,

"That is my brother, when he likes someone he will go for it."

I asked Miko,

"Do not you think your brother likes me?"

Miko replied,

"He loves you."

Our conversation ended when Haruhiko walked in. He sat down and asked me,

"How was Miko? Was she good company to be with?"

"Miko was an excellent hostess. You have a nice sister, Haruhiko."

We had lunch together without his parents and his sister. They seemed to reserve this moment for both of us. They ate downstairs so that Haruhiko and I could eat alone. I have come a long way, two thousand eight hundred miles to Tokyo, to see Haruhiko, their son.

After the weekend was over, I left Gunma-ken and Haruhiko to return to the Daiichi hotel in Tokyo on the Bullet Express Train, one of the fastest trains in the world. It took me less than two hours to get back to the city.

When the Japan Air Line (JAL) airplane was taking off the ground, I saw everything on the ground; city, highways, and office buildings. They grew smaller as the plane went higher. It left a deep sadness inside of me. I fell in love with Haruhiko. But how could I enjoy my life while millions of people in my South and North Vietnam were suffering with fighting and killing everyday.

XXXV

Troubled East India

Oudouman was a merchant from India who had lived many years in South Vietnam. He and his wife owned several large fabric stores in Saigon. He also was a big money changer of U. S. dollars and French francs. Oudouman and I, along with the girls in the international air travel office, were partners. We split the profit equally every time when we got a tourist or traveler from another part of the world that got a better exchange rate from us than from the bank. Oudouman needed the foreign exchange for many reasons. He needed to import larger purchases from outside of Vietnam. The foreign exchange rate at the government bank was very low and you could only exchange a limited amount. He invested his money in U. S. dollars to retain the value of his money in the Vietnamese market.

Everything was alright until he found out that his accountant was cheating on taxes for more than five years. When the Ministry of Interior called him to the office, he knew it was too late to do anything. He called me up and told me what was happening to him. He might need an air ticket for emergency leave. Within five days, he could be charged with five years in prison if he could not come up with the penalties for not paying the taxes he owed to the government. This amount was one hundred thousand U.S. dollars. This penalty could cause him to be imprisoned for ten years. Those five days enabled him time to gain exit to America. Since then his name was on the black list in all government offices. He insisted,

"Please do something about this. I know you know many government officials and airline employees. With a touch of your magic power, you can do it."

Oudouman summarized,

"If you only talk to people, you can motivate them and get them do things they normally would not do."

I had no other way to avoid him, he knew me too well. I must help Oudouman; he had been honest in business with me and my friends for a long time. I gave him two choices. I said,

"Would you like to take the sea or air?"

Oudouman grasped the rare opportunity and said,

"I want to go by air, once the plane is taking off the ground I have no fear of being arrested inside the plane. But, by sea, it takes a long time to get out of the area, and the chance to be caught is greater."

I told Oudouman,

"If you go by air, we must get you past the airport police gate. With their system, they will find your identity. I can make all connections at the airport. But do you mind spending some money?"

Oudouman replied immediately,

"Not at all. As long as I can get out of Vietnam as soon as possible, I will do whatever it takes. I will do anything you say,

Miss April. Please book me a ticket to any city in the United
States.

I responded,

"Alright, Mr. Oudouman, give me twenty-four hours to
confirm with you, and your departure. I need to talk to a couple
of people. You might have to give them a couple thousand
dollars each, so get your money ready, okay? I will talk to you
tomorrow. In these cases, money really talks."

I dialed the number. Brandy's voice came on,

"Hello, who is it?"

I asked,

"Sister Brandy, is your husband home?

Brandy said,

"No, he is not home. What is the emergency since you are
calling us this time of night? It is eleven in the evening.

Brandy was a typical housewife. She was one of the
reasons why her husband was corrupted. She liked to stick her

nose into her husband's business. You had to bribe her to get some information about where her husband was and get her to call him up for you. I said,

"Sister Brandy, I have two bottles of French perfume Chanel 5 to give you. I have a new deal for brother Bình, your husband and a grand for you to do shopping. I must talk to your husband before the morning breaks out."

Brandy replied with a hypocritical voice,

"Do not worry about money. We are friends of long standing. Just feel free to call here anytime. Let me get on the other line and speak to Bình that you are waiting to talk with him."

A couple minutes went by and perhaps Oudouman was worried to death from not hearing from me. Brandy's voice on the phone,

"April, please hang up. Tom will call you right back. Good luck, my friend. I will see you soon with the French perfume. It is my favorite.

393

The departure of Oudouman was arranged. Two computer operators at the airport had been paid to ignore Oudouman's identity. When it was Oudouman's turn, the computer operator skipped his name and said,

"Pass."

The police at the airport let Oudouman step inside the plane. His new life began once the plane took off from the airport.

His wife remained in Saigon with seven stores still in business. Oudouman was smart enough to license all their businesses in his wife's name. The law in Vietnam was that if Mr. Smith married Miss Jones, Miss Jones would retain her maiden name. This way, Oudouman was able to license all his business in his wife's name, which was Ms. Jones. By law, the Vietnamese government could not do anything to the properties of Ms. Jones. So the government prohibited Oudouman to return to Vietnam. When I broke the news to Oudouman's wife that his plane had already left Vietnam, she handed to me a doggy bag and said,

"This is your lunch bag, April, thank you."

After I got home and opened it, I found hundreds of dollars inside the bag for my forty-eight hours of tense work. We did business in Vietnam that way because of our life long existence and trustworthiness.

The risk to my safety and everyone else involved was enormous, but the satisfaction of knowing I helped those unfortunates was well worth it.

In spite of tight government securities in the city, Bernard managed to visit government offices as well as he did in the battlefields when South Vietnamese soldiers were fighting against the VCs or when the rockets hit the villages. He was a professional photographer and a movie maker for his own company. He lived in the city and many times he had to travel to where the real action was to shoot the movies. He photographed real scenes which the South Vietnamese government wanted to see.

Bernard was on a schedule for leaving the country with his productions. During his hard work, many times he nearly got killed in the many war zones, where he photographed. Bernard was of French and Vietnamese blood heritage. He grew up in South Vietnam and went to school in France.

The telephone rang, the voice on the other line, said,

"Bernard, this is the Commander-in-Chief of the South Vietnamese National Defense. I am interested in buying all your documentary films. Why don't you come to our headquarters and show us the films."

Bernard was twenty-eight. Something told him to be on guard to such phone calls and deals. Bernard questioned,

"How much would you give me for the films?"

"I can give you up to five hundred thousand U.S. Dollars. Can you do it this evening, Bernard?"

What else could be behind the deal, Bernard thought. So he said,

"I will be there, please give me the time you want me there, sir."

In the private auditorium of the National Defense the films were being shown. When all the movies were over, the Commander-in-Chief, started giving him a lecture, he states,

"Bernard, your films could cause chaos in the country and disintegration amongst our armies. For these reasons, all your films must remain in our headquarters."

The Commander-in-Chief continued,

"You have twenty four hour to get out of the country."

Bernard got inside the airport and headed toward the gate where he had been told to wait near the gate, where the passengers were getting off the plane and going inside. As it was arranged, the last couple passengers were leaving the plane and the air plane attendant said loudly,

"Sir, you left your bags inside the plane."

Bernard got the signal, he quickly said,

"Thanks."

Bernard stepped inside the plane and there he waited for a new beginning in the United States of America. I was his friend, who came to his rescue just in the nick of time. I remained temporarily in Vietnam with a good feeling, knowing I was able to help others to leave South Vietnam for safe life in the United States.

About the Author

She had many opportunities to become wealthy but chose not to. She was an unarmed Christian/Buddhist soldier without a prayer and without a church. She had conflicting ideas about life and people in general. Some of her ideas were fulfilled during the Vietnam conflict. She was an inspiration to those who had misfortune, and a joy for the affliction and healing for others. She was born and raised in a family where her mother was a Minister, an eye surgeon and a believer in God's faith. Her mother practiced that faith by offering her services to others for free. "She is the DOVE," her mother once said. She was the voice of the deaf and the eye of the blind. She is indispensable, dynamic, innovative and bright.

CPSIA information can be obtained
at www.ICGtesting.com
Printed in the USA
BVHW032254090121
597471BV00009B/120/J

9 781410 741363